The Room in the Dragon Volant

A Gothic Romance of Deception, Intrigue, and the Supernatural

A Modern Translation

Adapted for the Contemporary Reader

J. Sheridan Le Fanu

Translated by Tim Zengerink

Table of Contents

Preface - Message to the Reader

What If You Could Help Rebuild the Greatest Library in Human History?

Thousands of years ago, the Library of Alexandria stood as the crown jewel of human achievement — a sanctuary where the collected wisdom of every known civilization was gathered, preserved, and shared freely.

And then, it was lost.

Through fire, conquest, and the slow erosion of time, humanity lost not just books — but ideas, dreams, discoveries, and stories that could have changed the world forever.

Today, the Library of Alexandria lives again — and you are invited to be a part of its restoration.

Our mission is simple yet profound:

To rebuild the greatest library the world has ever known, and to translate all timeless works into every language and dialect, so that no seeker of knowledge is ever left behind again.

By joining our movement to rebuild the modern Library of Alexandria, you become part of an unprecedented mission:

- **Unlimited Access to the Greatest Audiobooks & eBooks Ever Written:**

  Instantly explore thousands of legendary works—Plato, Shakespeare, Jane Austen, Leo Tolstoy, and countless more. All instantly available to read or listen, placing a complete literary universe at your fingertips.

- **Beautiful Paperback & Deluxe Editions at Printing Cost**

  Own any title as an elegant paperback, deluxe hardcover, or stunning collectible boxset—offered to you at true printing cost, delivered straight to your door. Build your personal Library of Alexandria, crafted for beauty, built for durability, and worthy of proud display.

- **Fresh Translations for Modern Readers—in Every Language & Dialect**

  Enjoy timeless masterpieces reimagined in clear, contemporary language—no more outdated phrases or obscure references. Alongside the original versions, we're tirelessly translating these classics into every language and dialect imaginable, ensuring accessibility and understanding across cultures and generations.

- **Join a Global Renaissance of Literature & Knowledge**

  You directly support expanding our library, publishing deluxe editions at true cost, translating works into all global languages, and bringing humanity's greatest stories to people everywhere. By joining today, you're not just preserving a legacy of masterpieces; you set in motion a powerful wave of literary accessibility.

Become a Torchbearer of Knowledge.

Join us for free now at **LibraryofAlexandria.com**

Together, we will ensure that the light of human wisdom never fades again.

With gratitude and a shared love of knowledge,

The Modern Library of Alexandria Team

Visit:

www.libraryofalexandria.com

Or scan the code below:

Introduction

Romance, Deception,
and the Shadow of the Supernatural

J. Sheridan Le Fanu's The Room in the Dragon Volant, first published in 1872, is a masterful blend of gothic suspense, psychological intrigue, and subtle supernatural suggestion. Set against the backdrop of post-Napoleonic France, this novella-length tale diverges in tone and construction from some of Le Fanu's more overtly ghostly stories, such as Carmilla or Green Tea. Instead, it thrives in the space between the real and the unreal, in a liminal territory where rationality and fear war with desire, greed, and illusion. Combining elements of romantic adventure, gothic melodrama, and crime fiction, The Room in the Dragon Volant is both a compelling psychological study and a meticulously constructed tale of misdirection.

The story follows Richard Beckett, a young, impulsive Englishman traveling through France in pursuit of love, honor, and perhaps a little vanity. Enchanted by a mysterious countess he meets on the road, Beckett finds himself staying at the Dragon Volant, a secluded and shadowy inn whose reputation is cloaked in rumor. As he becomes entangled in a web of flirtation, conspiracy, and peril, Beckett is forced to confront not only external threats but also the vulnerabilities of his own romantic imagination. What unfolds is a tale that draws the reader ever deeper into an atmosphere of mounting suspense, where reality becomes increasingly elusive and danger hides behind every door—especially the locked one in the infamous room of the title.

Although The Room in the Dragon Volant contains no explicit ghost or specter, it is a gothic story through and through. Le Fanu excels in creating an ambiance of dread and ambiguity, where appearances are deceiving and safety is always illusory. The haunted nature of the inn, the cryptic behavior of its guests, and the ominous legends surrounding the titular room all serve to build a sense of inevitable doom. But what truly haunts this story is not a phantom—it is human greed, deceit, and the haunting failure of reason in the face of desire.

In this introduction, we will explore The Room in the Dragon Volant through three major lenses: its structural play with genre and reader expectation, its psychological depth and character dynamics, and its place in Le Fanu's broader literary legacy. By the end, it becomes clear that this is not just a tale of gothic intrigue, but a warning about self-deception, the fatal allure of appearances, and the razor-thin line between romance and ruin.

The Architecture of Suspense: Genre Subversion and Narrative Craft

One of the most distinctive features of The Room in the Dragon Volant is how carefully Le Fanu manipulates the reader's expectations. At first glance, the novella presents itself as a romantic adventure: a brave young hero meets a beautiful, tragic woman; a chivalrous romance is born; and the inn where he stays may be haunted by mysterious forces. The opening scenes of Beckett's journey, his gallant gestures, and his idealistic view of love all contribute to the illusion of a conventional romantic or chivalric narrative. This is a trap—both for the reader and for Beckett himself.

Le Fanu, however, is not interested in delivering a straightforward gothic romance. Instead, he constructs a story that slowly peels back its own façade. The romantic interest, the alluring Countess de St. Alyre, proves to be far more dangerous than she appears. The seeming coincidences that lead Beckett into the countess's confidence and into the infamous room of the Dragon Volant are not serendipitous but carefully orchestrated. Le Fanu's true subject is not the supernatural—it is illusion, and how easy it is for desire to be weaponized against the self.

The story's pacing is deliberate. Le Fanu builds suspense through a series of carefully planted clues, unexplained details, and increasingly unsettling observations. Each character is shrouded in ambiguity. The mysterious Marquis d'Harmonville, the duplicitous Count de St. Alyre, and even the seemingly loyal servants all contribute to an atmosphere of profound mistrust. Beckett, convinced that he is the hero of a romantic tale, fails to see that he is being manipulated at every turn.

Le Fanu's greatest triumph in the structure of the novella is the climactic twist—when the reader, along with Beckett, realizes the full scope of the conspiracy. The titular room, far from being the site of a ghostly haunting, is the scene of an elaborately staged crime—a place where wealthy victims are drugged, buried alive, and robbed. The terror that Beckett experiences while paralyzed and buried beneath the earth is not supernatural—it is visceral, physical, and utterly human.

This structural reversal is not a gimmick. It is the heart of Le Fanu's narrative strategy: to show that the most terrifying haunts are the ones created by human minds, and the most dangerous monsters wear beautiful faces and speak of love.

Self-Deception and the Perils of Desire

At the core of The Room in the Dragon Volant lies a character study of Richard Beckett—a man whose intellect is subverted by his imagination, whose judgment is clouded by romance, and whose downfall is ultimately brought about by his own idealism. Unlike many gothic protagonists who are menaced by external forces, Beckett's most formidable enemy is himself.

Beckett is no fool in the traditional sense. He is educated, brave, and earnest. But his vision of the world is hopelessly romantic, shaped by novels, illusions of chivalry, and a belief in the redemptive power of love. This vision makes him blind to manipulation, deaf to warnings, and incapable of discerning reality from performance. The Countess de St. Alyre, with her veil of sorrow and her cryptic charm, becomes the object of his infatuation—not because of who she is, but because of what she represents to him: a damsel in distress, a chance for heroic purpose.

Le Fanu uses this dynamic to explore a deeper theme: the danger of projecting fantasies onto others, and the ease with which passion can override reason. Beckett wants the world to fit his narrative, and others exploit this desire. His downfall is not simply a case of mistaken trust—it is the inevitable result of refusing to see people as they are.

When the truth is revealed and Beckett narrowly escapes death, he is forced to reckon with his own gullibility. His romanticism, once a source of hope, is now a source of shame. The lesson he learns is brutal but necessary: that the heart, unmoored from reason, can become a path to ruin.

This psychological realism is what elevates the story beyond gothic theatrics. Le Fanu does not give us a villain to defeat or a ghost to banish. He gives us a protagonist who must confront himself. The real horror is not what Beckett finds in the Dragon Volant, but what he learns about his own mind—and how easily it betrayed him.

Between Ghosts and Graveyards:
Le Fanu's Gothic Realism

Though The Room in the Dragon Volant contains no ghost in the traditional sense, it is deeply haunted. Haunted by atmosphere, by history, by deception, and by the inevitability of death. The inn, with its secret passages and deadly room, serves as a gothic symbol of entrapment and illusion. The tomb where Beckett is buried alive becomes the ultimate image of helplessness, a place where romantic dreams go to die.

Le Fanu, a master of gothic literature, understood that fear does not require the supernatural. His best work—Carmilla, Uncle Silas, The Familiar—thrives in the spaces between reality and imagination. In The Room in the Dragon Volant, he eschews ghosts in favor of the human capacity for cruelty and deception. He shows that the gothic is not about external phantoms—it is about internal darkness.

Still, the story retains a spectral quality. The countess, though not a ghost, haunts the narrative with her duplicity. The inn, though not cursed, feels cursed by the crimes committed within it. And Beckett, though he survives, is marked forever by the experience—his innocence dead, his illusions shattered.

In this way, Le Fanu contributes to the evolution of gothic fiction. He moves the genre away from castles and curses and toward psychological horror. He anticipates the modern thriller, the noir detective story, and the domestic suspense novel. And he does so without losing the atmosphere, dread, and moral complexity that define the gothic tradition.

The Room in the Dragon Volant is not merely a mystery. It is a meditation on perception, trust, and the perilous gap between who we think we are and who we truly become when tested.

In the end, Beckett escapes—but he is not saved. And the Dragon Volant remains, its rooms ready, its secrets undisturbed, waiting for the next soul who dares to mistake danger for romance.

Prologue

The strange story I'm about to share is mentioned several times—very clearly—in a fascinating essay written by Doctor Hesselius. The essay is about the mysterious drugs used during the Dark and Middle Ages.

He calls the essay Mortis Imago, and in it, he talks about old potions like Vinum letiferum, Beatifica, Somnus Angelorum, Hypnus Sagarum, Aqua Thessalliae, and around twenty more. These were well-known to wise men about eight hundred years ago. He also claims that two of them are still known—and even used—by criminals today, which sometimes gets revealed during police investigations.

The essay Mortis Imago is expected to take up two full volumes—volumes nine and ten—of Dr. Martin Hesselius's collected works.

It's filled with a surprising number of quotes from old poems and stories, mostly from medieval times. Strangely, some of the most important ones are actually from ancient Egypt.

Out of many cases like this one, I've chosen this story because it stands out—not just for what happened, but because it works well as a story. Since this is being published in an informal way, I'm sharing it simply as a tale.

Chapter I.
On the Road

In the important year of 1815, I was twenty-three years old and had just inherited a large sum of money in government bonds and other investments. Napoleon had just been defeated, and the continent was open again for English travelers eager to explore Europe. Once the short return of Napoleon, known as the "Hundred Days," ended with his defeat at Waterloo, I joined the many others heading to Paris.

I was traveling from Brussels to Paris, likely on the same road the allied army had marched just weeks earlier. There were so many carriages on the road that the dust stretched as far as the eye could see. Everywhere, tired horses were being led back to their posts at inns, having just finished one trip after another. It felt like the whole world was heading to Paris.

I didn't pay much attention to the scenery because my thoughts were full of dreams about Paris. But I do remember that about four miles outside a small town—whose name I've forgotten—we came across a carriage in trouble.

It hadn't crashed, but the two front horses had collapsed. The drivers had gotten down, and two servants were trying—without much success—to help. A pretty little bonnet peeked out the window of the carriage. I saw the bonnet and the shape of the woman's shoulders, and it was enough to make me want to help. I stopped my own carriage and jumped out to assist.

Unfortunately, the lady in the bonnet wore a thick black veil. I couldn't see her face, just the lace of the veil. A thin older man also leaned out of the window. He looked sickly and wore a black scarf up to his ears and nose, which he pulled down briefly to thank me excitedly in French.

One of my few talents—besides boxing, which every Englishman learned—was speaking French. I answered him politely, and after some friendly bowing, his head disappeared back into the carriage, and the bonnet appeared again.

The lady must have heard me talking to my servant because she spoke in charming, broken English. Her voice was so sweet, I felt even more frustrated that the veil was hiding her face.

I noticed the family crest painted on the carriage door. It was unusual—there was a red stork standing on one leg and holding a stone in the other. I later learned this symbol meant "vigilance." It stuck with me. The fancy carriage, the elegant servants, and the way they carried themselves made it clear they were nobility.

The mystery lady became even more interesting because of that. People may say it's shallow, but a title adds a special charm. Even a milkmaid is more impressed by a passing lord than by a lifetime of kindness from a regular man. That's just how the world is.

But this wasn't only about her status. I knew I was good-looking—tall, fit, and confident. So why did she thank me personally? Her companion had already done so. I had the feeling she was watching me with interest from behind her veil, and I felt her gaze.

Her carriage drove away, raising a trail of dust behind it. I watched it go, sighing like someone caught in a dream.

I told my driver not to pass them but to follow that carriage wherever it stopped. Eventually, we reached a small town, and they stopped at a cozy inn called the Belle Étoile. They got out and went inside.

I followed at a casual pace, pretending not to care. I peeked into a couple of rooms but didn't see them, so I headed upstairs. One room had its door open. I went in as if by accident.

It was a big, empty room—except for one person. She wore the same bonnet. Her back was to me, and she was reading a letter. I didn't know if her veil was still down, but I watched, hoping she might turn around.

Instead, she moved to stand in front of a mirror above a small table. In the reflection, I saw a woman so beautiful she could've been a painting. Her face was soft, sad, and lovely, with a hint of something mysterious. Her head was bowed, her long eyelashes and smooth eyebrows casting shadows as she read the letter.

She was perfectly still, like a statue. I could even see the blue veins in her pale neck.

I should've quietly left the room, but I was too fascinated. Then, suddenly, she raised her eyes. They were large and violet-colored, filled with sadness and pride. Our eyes met in the mirror.

She quickly pulled down her veil and turned away. I thought maybe she hoped I hadn't really seen her. But I had, and I couldn't look away. Every tiny movement of hers held my full attention.

Chapter II.
The Inn-Yard of the Belle Étoile

Her face was the kind that could make you fall in love in a second. Those strong emotions that take over young men hit me hard. I suddenly felt nervous and unsure of myself, and I started to think that maybe I didn't belong in that room at all. She cleared that up quickly. In the same sweet voice I'd heard earlier—but now colder and in French—she said, "Sir, perhaps you don't realize this is a private room."

I quickly bowed, apologized awkwardly, and backed toward the door.

I must have looked embarrassed, because I definitely felt it. Then, in a much softer voice, she added, "Still, I'm glad I got the chance to thank you again for your quick and kind help today."

Her change in tone gave me hope. She didn't have to recognize me, and even if she did, she wasn't required to thank me again. It was a small gesture, but it meant a lot—especially right after asking me to leave.

Her voice now sounded shy and quiet, and I noticed she glanced toward another door in the room. I wondered if the man in the black wig—maybe her jealous husband—was about to walk in. Right then, I heard a sharp, nasal voice shouting orders at a servant. It was the same voice that had loudly thanked me from the carriage window earlier.

"Please go," the lady said softly, gently motioning toward the door I came through.

I bowed again and stepped out, closing the door behind me.

I walked downstairs, feeling excited and happy. I found the innkeeper of the Belle Étoile, where I was staying, and described the room I had just left. I told him I liked it and asked if I could book it.

He looked uncomfortable. That room, and two others nearby, were already taken.

"By whom?" I asked.

"Important guests," he replied.

"But who are they? Surely they gave names or titles?"

"Of course, sir, but so many people are coming through on their way to Paris that we've stopped asking. We just call them by their room numbers now."

"How long will they stay?"

"I don't know, sir. It doesn't matter to us. The rooms never stay empty for long."

"I really would've liked those rooms! Is one of them a bedroom?"

"Yes, and as you know, people don't usually book bedrooms unless they're staying overnight."

"Well, are there any rooms left at all? I'll take anything."

"Yes, sir. Two rooms are still available."

I booked them right away.

It was clear these mysterious guests were staying at least until morning. I started to feel like I'd stepped into something exciting.

I moved into my rooms and looked out the window, which faced the inn's busy yard. Tired horses were being unhitched, and fresh ones were brought from the stables. Many carriages—some private, some like mine—were lined up, waiting for new horses. Servants rushed around while others stood around chatting or laughing. The whole scene was busy but fun to watch.

Among all the movement, I thought I saw the carriage and one of the servants belonging to the mysterious guests I'd become so curious about.

I rushed downstairs and slipped out the back door. In moments, I was out on the bumpy stone path in the middle of all the noise and activity. The sun was almost down, and golden light lit up the red brick chimneys. Two barrels on tall poles, used as pigeon houses, glowed like they were on fire. Everything looked beautiful in that light—even the ordinary things suddenly felt magical.

After a bit of searching, I found the exact carriage I'd been looking for. A servant was locking one of the doors—it had its own lock and key. I paused nearby, staring at the crest on the panel.

"That red stork is a nice design," I said, pointing to the shield. "It must belong to an important family."

The servant glanced at me as he slid the small key into his pocket and replied with a slight smirk and a polite bow, "Monsieur is free to guess."

Not discouraged, I offered a little tip—that classic trick to get people talking.

The servant looked at the coin in his hand, then up at me, clearly surprised. "Monsieur is very generous!"

"It's nothing," I said casually. "But can you tell me who the gentleman and lady are? The ones in this carriage? My servant and I helped them earlier when their horses fell."

"They're the Count and the young lady we call the Countess— though she might be his daughter. I'm not sure."

"Do you know where they live?"

"Honestly, sir, I don't. I was hired in Brussels the same day we left. I don't know much."

"You don't know where your own master lives? Don't you know anything more than his name?"

"Nothing that's worth much, sir. The Count's personal servant, Monsieur Picard, has been with him for years and knows everything. But he only talks when he's giving orders. I haven't learned a thing from him. We're going to Paris soon, and I'll probably find out more there. But for now, I'm just as in the dark as you."

"Where is this Monsieur Picard?"

"He's gone to get his razors sharpened. But I doubt he'll tell you anything."

That wasn't much to show for my money. I believed the servant was telling the truth—he probably would've shared secrets if he'd known any. I politely said goodbye and headed back up to my room.

I called for my servant. Although I had brought him from England, he was French—clever, quick, and very familiar with the tricks of his countrymen.

"St. Clair, close the door and come here. I can't relax until I find out more about the people staying in the rooms below mine. Here's fifteen francs—track down the servants we helped today, treat them to a little dinner and wine, and then come back and tell me everything they say. I just spoke to one of them who knows nothing. The other, the nobleman's personal valet, knows it all. That's the one you need to talk to. It's the old man I'm curious about, not the young lady. Got it? Now go! And come back with every detail you can."

It was the perfect job for St. Clair. I had gotten used to speaking to him in the familiar tone you find in old French plays, where masters and servants talk almost like friends.

I'm sure he laughed about it in private, but he was always respectful to my face.

He gave me a few wise looks, nods, and shrugs, then left. From my window, I saw him rush into the courtyard and disappear among the carriages.

Chapter III.
Death and Love Together Mated

When a day feels like it's crawling by and you're stuck alone, full of impatience and nerves, even the smallest things feel unbearable. Time seems to freeze—the minute hand of your watch moves as slowly as the hour hand once did, and the hour hand might as well not be moving at all. You find yourself yawning, tapping your fingers in frustration, pressing your face against the window, and humming tunes you don't even like. You're restless, bored, and can't think of anything to do. It's a shame you can't have a big, proper three-course dinner more than once a day. The rules of nature just won't allow it.

Back then, though, supper was still a solid meal, and its time was getting close. That was something to look forward to. Still, I had forty-five minutes to kill. What was I supposed to do?

I had a few books with me, but I wasn't in the mood to read. My novel sat on the sofa with my coat and walking stick, but I couldn't care less about what happened to the main characters—they could both drown in the rain barrel outside for all I cared. I paced back and forth in my room, sighed at my reflection, and fixed up my clothes. I adjusted my large white cravat, folded and tied like Beau Brummel used to wear. I put on my buff-colored waistcoat and my blue coat with shiny gold buttons. I soaked my handkerchief with Eau-de-Cologne (this was before the many perfumes we have now). I styled my hair carefully—it was thick, dark brown, and had a nice natural wave back then. Now it's all white, and my scalp is pink and bald, but let's not dwell on that. Back then, my hair was something I was proud of.

I finished dressing with a stylish hat, light French gloves, and a knobby walking stick that had recently become trendy in England. All this effort just to hang around the yard or sit on the steps of the Belle Étoile inn. But the truth was, I did it for her—the mysterious lady with the unforgettable eyes I had seen earlier that evening. I hoped, vaguely, that she might see me again and take note of how well I presented myself.

As I finished getting ready, the sun finally disappeared, leaving only a bit of fading twilight. I sighed, feeling the mood of the hour, and opened my window to get a breath of air. Right away, I realized the window below mine was also open. I heard two people talking, though I couldn't make out the words.

One voice stood out—it was high-pitched and nasal. I recognized it immediately as the man who had shouted thanks from the carriage earlier. The second voice was much softer and sweeter—hers. They didn't seem to be arguing, just having a calm conversation. Still, I selfishly wished they were fighting, so I could swoop in like a hero.

Then she started to sing.

You can always hear singing more clearly than speaking, and I could make out the words. Her voice was gentle and low, probably what they call a semi-contralto. It was beautiful, but also a little haunting. The song went something like this:

Death and Love hide side by side,
Waiting quietly for the right time.
It doesn't matter if it's day or night—
They'll find someone to make theirs.

One can chill you, one can burn,
Both can twist your thoughts and heart.

One might stop your life completely,
The other might just break it apart.

"Enough, madame!" snapped the old man's voice. "We are not here to entertain the stable hands with music!"

She laughed in reply, bright and careless.

"You want a fight, madame!" he said sharply. Then I heard the window slam shut with a loud bang that could have shattered the glass.

Glass might be thin, but it's great at blocking sound. After that, I couldn't hear anything—not even a whisper.

What a voice she had! The way it rose and fell—it was magical. It moved me. And to think some grumpy old man could silence that lovely voice with a single outburst! "What a life," I thought. "That beautiful woman, with the grace of a goddess and the talents of a muse, stuck in such a cage. She knew I was above her—she must've heard my window open. I wonder who that song was meant for. I bet the old man thought the same thing."

Still caught up in my thoughts, I left my room and walked slowly past the Count's door, hoping—just maybe—that she would come out. I even dropped my walking stick right by their door and took my time picking it up. But no luck. I couldn't hang around all night, so I made my way downstairs.

I checked the clock. Only fifteen minutes left until supper.

Everything was chaos at the inns these days. People were packed in everywhere. So, maybe—just maybe—the Count and Countess would join the others at the shared dinner table tonight.

Chapter IV.
Monsieur Droqville

Full of excitement and hope, I stepped out onto the steps of the Belle Étoile. Night had fallen, and the moonlight made everything look soft and magical. Ever since I arrived, I'd let myself get swept up in this romantic adventure. The moonlight made it all feel even more dreamy. I couldn't help thinking: what if she's the Count's daughter—and falls in love with me? Or worse—what if she's his wife? That would be a beautiful tragedy.

While I stood there, deep in thought, a tall, well-dressed man approached me. He looked about fifty, carried himself gracefully, and had the air of someone very important. It was hard not to think he was someone of high rank.

He had also been standing there, quietly admiring the moonlit street, and now turned to me with the kind, confident politeness of an old-fashioned French nobleman. He asked if I was Mr. Beckett. I said yes, and he introduced himself in a low voice as the Marquis d'Harmonville. Then he said he had a letter for me from Lord R——, who knew my father a little and had once done me a small favor.

This Lord R—— was a major figure in politics, rumored to be the next English ambassador to Paris. I bowed and read the letter:

My dear Beckett,

I want to introduce you to my close friend, the Marquis d'Harmonville. He'll tell you more about how you might be able to help him—and help us, too.

The Marquis is wealthy, well-connected to old noble families, and respected by the royal court. He's working with us quietly, as requested by both his king and ours.

Also—Walton mentioned yesterday that your seat might be at risk. There's something happening at Domwell. I can't step in personally, but maybe you could have Haxton look into it and send a report. It sounds like it could be serious.

One last thing: for personal reasons, the Marquis is going by the name "Monsieur Droqville" for the next few weeks. Everyone involved is aware of this.

I'm heading into town now.

Yours,

R——

I was completely confused. I barely knew Lord R——. I didn't know anyone named Haxton, and the only Walton I knew was my hatter. But the letter spoke as if we were close friends. Then I looked at the outside of the envelope and my heart dropped.

It was addressed to George Stanhope Beckett, Esq., M.P.

That wasn't me. I was just Richard Beckett.

I looked at the Marquis in shock. "I'm so sorry," I said. "My name is Beckett, and I do know Lord R——but only a little. This letter isn't meant for me. It's for Mr. Stanhope Beckett, the Member of Parliament. I swear I didn't know. Please believe me when I say I'll keep everything I read in strict confidence."

I must have looked truly embarrassed, because the Marquis's serious face softened, and he smiled. He held out his hand.

"I believe you," he said. "And if this mistake had to happen, I'm glad it was with a man of honor. May I count you as a friend?"

I thanked him, genuinely moved. Then he added:

"If you'd ever like to visit me at my home in Claironville, Normandy, on August 15, I'll be hosting many guests you might enjoy meeting."

I thanked him again. He continued, "Right now, I can't see visitors at my home in Paris, for reasons I'm sure you understand. But let me know which hotel you'll be staying at, and I'll make sure Monsieur Droqville keeps in touch."

I gave him my hotel details, and he added, "If you ever think of a way I can help you, just let me know."

I felt truly flattered. Maybe the Marquis wanted to stay friendly just to keep me quiet, but still—it felt like the beginning of a real connection. He then said goodnight and headed back inside the inn.

I stayed on the steps, thinking about it all. But soon, the memory of her face, voice, and presence came back stronger than anything. I looked up at the moon and walked slowly along the quiet streets, deep in thought.

Later, I wandered back into the now quiet inn-yard. It was peaceful compared to the chaos earlier. The servants were probably eating dinner. I didn't mind the quiet. I walked up to her carriage, which sat quietly in the moonlight. I walked around it, lost in a silly daydream. I imagined how many times she must've looked at that same coat of arms on the door.

Suddenly, a loud voice behind me broke the silence.

"A red stork—how fitting. The stork's a greedy bird. Always watching. Always hunting. Blood red! Quite the symbol."

I turned and saw the palest face I'd ever seen—wide, harsh, and cruel. He wore an officer's uniform and was at least six feet tall. A deep scar ran across his eyebrow and nose.

He chuckled in a low, mean way. "I once shot a stork out of the sky just for fun," he said. "You see, when a man like me—smart, sharp, experienced—decides to uncover a secret, expose a crime, or run a thief through with a sword, it's going to happen. Ha! Goodbye, sir."

He spun on his heel and marched off into the night.

Chapter V.
Supper at the Belle Étoile

The French army was in a bad mood at the time, especially toward the English. It was clear, though, that the angry man who had just criticized the Count's carriage crest wasn't upset with me. He seemed lost in his own bitter memories and had stormed off, still fuming.

Still, I had that uncomfortable feeling you get when you realize someone has been watching you while you thought you were alone. It was worse this time because of how unpleasant the man looked and how close he had been—almost in my face. His strange, angry words were still echoing in my head. At least it gave me more to think about, especially as someone who was already deeply interested in the mysterious Countess.

It was time for dinner. I wondered if I might hear anything useful at the table. Maybe some conversation would shed light on the people I was so curious about.

I walked into the dining room and scanned the crowd of about thirty people. With so many guests and so little help, it wasn't easy to get meals served privately, so a lot of people who normally wouldn't have eaten with strangers had no choice but to join the table.

The Count and the lady weren't there. But I was surprised to see the Marquis d'Harmonville, who I didn't expect in such a public space. He smiled and motioned to an empty seat beside him. I took it, and he seemed happy I did.

"Is this your first time in France?" he asked.

I said yes, and he replied, "I hope I don't seem nosy, but Paris is one of the most dangerous cities for a young, kindhearted man to visit alone. If you're not traveling with someone who knows the ropes…"

He didn't finish, but I told him I had no guide, just my own experience and common sense. I'd seen enough of life in England to handle myself, and I figured people were the same everywhere.

He shook his head with a smile. "You'll find people are very different. Every country has its own way of thinking and behaving. And that even shows in the way people commit crimes. In Paris, the number of people who live by scamming others is three or four times higher than in London. And they live better—some live in luxury. They're smarter, more creative, and have more flair than English crooks. They're good actors. These talents make them dangerous. They can pass as high-society folks with expensive homes, stylish clothes, and refined manners. Even local Parisians are fooled."

He leaned closer. "Their homes are full of rich decor, and important visitors from abroad often stop by. Some foolish young noblemen fall for it, too. These people host card games and invite guests. The man and woman who live there don't play themselves. They just set the stage for their partners to cheat and steal from the guests."

"But I've heard of an Englishman—a Lord Rooksbury's son—who beat the gamblers at their own game last year," I said.

He laughed. "So you're here to do the same, are you? I tried something like that when I was your age. I started with half a million francs and thought I could win big by doubling my bets. I'd heard that strategy would always work—just keep doubling until you win."

He chuckled again. "But the casino was ready for me. They had rules in place to stop that kind of thing. You weren't allowed to double more than four times in a row. They knew all the tricks, and I lost before I even got started."

"Is that rule still in place?" I asked, disappointed.

He laughed and shrugged. "Of course it is, my young friend. People who make a living doing something always understand it better than someone new to it. I can tell you had the same idea. You probably came well-prepared."

I admitted I had brought an even larger amount of money—I had thirty thousand pounds ready to play with.

"Anyone connected to my good friend, Lord R———, is someone I care about," he said warmly. "And I already like you. So I hope you'll forgive me if I've been a little too forward with my questions and advice."

I thanked him sincerely for his advice and asked him to please keep sharing any guidance he could.

"Then take my advice," he said seriously, "and leave your money in the bank. Don't gamble a single coin in those gaming houses. The night I went in to break the bank, I lost almost eight thousand pounds in one evening. After that, I was invited to one of those fancy gambling houses that pretend to be private homes owned by rich people. I was lucky to be saved from disaster by a gentleman I've respected ever since. Strangely enough, he's staying at this very inn. I saw his servant and went to visit him. He's still the same brave, kind, and honorable man I knew back then. If he weren't living such a quiet life now, I would definitely introduce you. Fifteen years ago, he would have been the best person you could talk to. His name is the Comte de St. Alyre. He comes from a very old and respected family. He's a man of honor and incredibly wise—except in one area."

"And what is that?" I asked, curious.

"He married a beautiful young woman who is at least forty-five years younger than he is," the Marquis said. "And now, even though I'm sure she's never given him a reason to doubt her, he's horribly jealous."

"And the lady?" I asked.

"The Countess is, as far as I know, completely worthy of him," he answered with a hint of reserve. "I believe I heard her singing this evening."

"Yes, I think so too. She's very talented," I said.

We were quiet for a moment before he added, "I must keep an eye on you. I'd hate for the next time you see Lord R—— to involve you telling him you were tricked in Paris. You're a young, wealthy Englishman, with a large sum waiting for you at a Paris bank. You're kind, lively, and generous—just the kind of person all the crooks and scammers are eager to trap."

Just then, the man sitting on my other side bumped into me. It was probably by accident as he turned in his seat.

"On my honor as a soldier, no one here heals as fast as I do!" he shouted in a loud, rough voice that startled me.

I turned and saw the same officer with the pale face who had unnerved me earlier in the inn yard. He wiped his mouth roughly and took a big gulp of wine before continuing.

"It's not blood in me—it's magic! Cut me, shoot me, blow me up, and I'll be back on my feet before your tailor could sew a button!

Gentlemen, if you saw me without my shirt, you'd laugh. Look at this hand—saber cut right through the palm to the bone. Stitched up with three stitches, and five days later I was playing ball with an English general in a prison yard in Madrid!"

He slapped the table and leaned forward, getting louder.

"At Arcola, now that was a battle! We all breathed so much smoke in five minutes, it could've choked this entire room. I was hit with two musket balls in the thighs, a grape shot in the calf, a lance in my shoulder, a piece of shrapnel in my arm, a bayonet in my ribs, and a huge gash on my chest—and a rocket to the forehead, for good measure! Not bad, right? Eight days later I was marching barefoot, cheering my company on, good as new!"

"Bravo! Bravissimo!" shouted a short, excited Italian man across the table. "Your story should be written in blood! All of Europe must hear it!"

"That was nothing!" the soldier shouted. "At Ligny, just the other day, I got hit by shell fragments that sliced open my leg and hit an artery. Blood was spraying like a fountain! I would've died in a minute, but I whipped off my sash, tied it above the wound, yanked a bayonet from a dead Prussian, twisted it tight like a tourniquet—and saved my own life! But I lost so much blood, I've looked pale ever since. Doesn't matter. It was worth it!"

Then he calmly returned to his wine as if nothing unusual had just been said.

The Marquis had shut his eyes and looked annoyed and fed up during all that shouting.

"Waiter," said the officer quietly for the first time, leaning over the back of his chair, "who arrived in that yellow and black carriage out in the yard? The one with the fancy symbols on the door and the red stork—red as my uniform?"

The waiter said he didn't know.

Then the officer, who had suddenly become serious and no longer seemed interested in chatting with the rest of the group, let his eyes rest on me—almost like by accident.

"Excuse me, sir," he said. "Didn't I see you looking at that carriage earlier? Can you tell me who it belongs to?"

"I think it's the Count and Countess de St. Alyre," I replied.

"They're staying here at the Belle Étoile?" he asked quickly.

"They've taken rooms upstairs," I said.

He jumped up suddenly, almost knocking his chair over, then sat back down just as fast. I could hear him cursing under his breath and mumbling to himself, sometimes smirking, other times frowning. I couldn't tell if he was scared or angry.

I turned to say something to the Marquis, but he had already left. A few other guests had left too, and before long the whole dinner party had broken up. A few thick logs were still glowing in the fireplace—it had turned chilly outside. I settled into a big wooden armchair with a very tall back that looked like it was hundreds of years old.

"Waiter," I said, "do you know who that officer is?"

"That's Colonel Gaillarde, sir."

"Has he stayed here before?"

"Yes, once. For a week, about a year ago."

"He's the palest person I've ever seen."

"That's true, sir. People sometimes think he's a ghost."

"Can you bring me a bottle of really good Burgundy?"

"The best in France, sir."

"Put it and a glass on this table, please. I might sit here for half an hour."

"Of course, sir."

I was completely relaxed. The wine was amazing, and my thoughts were warm and full of hope. "Beautiful Countess," I thought, "will we ever get to know each other better?"

Chapter VI.
The Naked Sword

A man who's been traveling all day, breathing different air every half hour, feeling pleased with himself, with no worries, and sitting in a cozy chair by the fire after a big meal—well, it's no surprise if he nods off.

I had just poured my fourth glass of wine when I fell asleep. My head probably lolled at an awkward angle, and all those rich French dishes didn't exactly help me have sweet dreams.

While relaxing in the inn, I had a strange dream. I imagined I was in a giant cathedral lit only by four candles, one at each corner of a raised platform covered in black cloth. Lying on it, also draped in black, was what looked like the dead body of the Countess de St. Alyre. The air was cold, the cathedral felt empty, and I could only see a short distance around me in the candlelight.

What I did see looked very old and gloomy, and my imagination filled in the darkness with haunting shapes. Then I heard the slow footsteps of two people walking down the stone aisle. The faint echoes gave a sense of how huge the place was. A terrible feeling of fear and suspense took over me. I was frozen in place when I suddenly heard the body on the platform whisper, "They're coming to bury me alive; save me."

I couldn't move. I couldn't speak. I was terrified.

Out of the darkness came the two figures. One was the Count de St. Alyre. He quietly moved to the head of the body and slipped his long, pale hands under it. The other was the pale-faced colonel with the scar, looking evil and satisfied. He took hold of her feet. Together, they started to lift her.

With all my strength, I finally broke free from the fear that held me still and jumped to my feet, gasping.

I was wide awake now—but Colonel Gaillarde was sitting across the fireplace from me, his face pale and staring at me like death itself.

"Where is she?" I blurted out.

"That depends," he said coldly, "on who she is."

"Good heavens," I muttered, glancing around in confusion.

The Colonel looked amused. He had just finished his small cup of black coffee and was sipping his brandy.

"I must have been dreaming," I said, trying to excuse any strange words I might've said aloud. "I wasn't sure where I was for a minute."

"You're the young man staying in the rooms above the Count and Countess de St. Alyre, aren't you?" he asked, squinting one eye and watching me closely with the other.

"I believe so—yes," I answered.

"Well, kid," he said with a smirk, "you'd better hope your dreams don't get any worse." He gave a slow nod and chuckled. "Worse dreams," he said again.

"What do you mean, Colonel?" I asked.

"I'm trying to figure that out myself," he replied. "And I think I will. Once I get the smallest bit of the truth in my grip, I don't let go. I follow it little by little, winding it up until I've got the whole thing. Clever, sneaky, sharp as a weasel! If I'd gone into spying, I'd be rich by now." He glanced at my wine bottle. "Is that stuff any good?"

"Very," I said. "Would the Colonel like a glass?"

He grabbed the biggest glass available, filled it to the top, raised it with a nod, and took a slow drink.

"Bah! That's not real Burgundy," he scoffed, making a face and pouring more. "You should've let me order your wine. They brought you the cheap stuff."

I politely escaped from the conversation and went outside with just my walking stick for company. I wandered into the yard and looked up at the Countess's windows. They were shut. I couldn't even see a light—no glimpse of her reading, writing, or just thinking, even if it wasn't about me.

I tried to bear the disappointment and took a slow walk through the town. I won't bore you with moonlight descriptions or poetic ramblings of a man who's fallen for a beautiful stranger. Let's just say I walked around for about half an hour and then took a slightly different path back.

That's when I ended up in a small square with a few tall, old houses on each side and a worn-out stone statue in the middle. A man was standing in front of the statue, looking at it. I recognized him right away—it was the Marquis d'Harmonville. He spotted me too.

He walked over, shrugged, and chuckled. "Surprised to see Monsieur Droqville staring at a stone figure by moonlight? I'll do anything to pass the time. You look bored too. These little towns are so dull! I love the friend who brought me here, but this place makes me question that friendship."

"You're heading to Paris in the morning?" I asked.

"I've ordered horses," I said.

"I'm waiting for a letter or someone to show up—either would let me leave, but I don't know when that'll be."

"Is there any way I can help?"

"No, thank you a thousand times. This is a performance where all the roles are already filled. I'm just here as a favor to a friend."

We walked slowly toward the Belle Étoile as he kept talking. Then there was a pause, and I asked, "Do you know anything about Colonel Gaillarde?"

"Oh yes, of course," he said. "He's a bit crazy—he had some serious head injuries. He used to annoy the War Office constantly with his wild ideas. He always believes in some fantasy. They gave him some kind of job, not in a real regiment. But during this last campaign, Napoleon needed everyone, so he gave him command of a regiment. He's always been a fierce fighter—and they really needed people like that."

There was—or used to be—another inn in the town called the Écu de France. The Marquis stopped in front of it, said good night in a mysterious way, and vanished inside.

As I slowly walked back toward my inn, I passed under a row of poplar trees and spotted the same waiter who had brought me my Burgundy earlier. I had Colonel Gaillarde on my mind, so I stopped him.

"You said Colonel Gaillarde stayed at the Belle Étoile for a week once, right?"

"Yes, Monsieur."

"Is he... all there? In his right mind?"

The waiter looked at me, surprised. "Completely, Monsieur."

"He's never been thought of as crazy?"

"Never, Monsieur. He's loud, but very clever."

"What am I supposed to think?" I muttered, continuing on my way.

Soon I was close enough to see the lights of the Belle Étoile. A carriage with four horses stood waiting in the moonlight at the door, and from inside, I heard shouting—especially the loud, furious voice of Colonel Gaillarde.

Most young men are drawn to a good scene, and somehow, I knew this one was going to be especially important to me. I ran the short distance and stepped into the inn's hallway.

There, in the middle of the chaos, was the Colonel himself. He was facing the Count de St. Alyre, who was dressed for travel. His face was partially hidden behind a black silk scarf. It looked like he had been trying to reach his carriage but had been stopped. Behind him, the Countess stood in her travel clothes, her black veil covering her face, and a white rose in her hand.

The Colonel looked completely out of control. His face was twisted with rage, the veins on his forehead bulging, eyes wild, teeth clenched, and even froth on his lips. He had drawn his sword and was waving it while yelling furiously and stamping his feet.

The innkeeper was trying to calm him down, but it wasn't working. Two waiters stood back, pale and too afraid to move. The Colonel kept shouting, swinging his sword, and yelling things like:

"I wasn't sure about your red stork, your symbol of blood! I couldn't believe you'd dare to travel openly on public roads, staying in inns with honest men. You two—monsters! Vampires, werewolves, ghouls! Call the police, I say! If either of you try to walk out that door, I'll take your heads off!"

I stood frozen for a moment. What a scene this was. Then I walked straight to the Countess. She grabbed my arm, clearly shaken.

"Oh, Monsieur," she whispered anxiously. "That terrible madman! What are we going to do? He won't let us leave—he'll kill my husband."

"Don't worry, Madame," I said bravely, stepping in between the Count and the Colonel, who was still yelling. I shouted at him, "Shut your mouth and get out of the way, you thug, you bully, you coward!"

The lady gave a soft cry, which, in that moment, felt like a reward for my boldness. The Colonel paused for a second, stunned—then his sword flashed in the air as he swung to strike me down.

Chapter VII.
The White Rose

I was too fast for Colonel Gaillarde. As he raised his sword, ready to strike me down, I hit him on the side of the head with my heavy stick. He stumbled, and I hit him again in the same spot. This time, he collapsed and didn't move—he looked like he might be dead.

I honestly didn't care if he was. I was overwhelmed with a mix of excitement, triumph, and even a bit of darkness.

I stepped on his sword and broke it in two, then tossed the pieces into the street. The old Count de St. Alyre didn't look back or thank anyone. He simply rushed across the floor, out the door, and into his carriage.

That left the Countess standing alone. I immediately offered her my arm, which she took, and I led her to the carriage. She got in, and I closed the door behind her. We didn't speak a word.

I leaned toward the open window, about to ask if she needed anything from me. Her hand gently touched mine, her lips close to my cheek, and she whispered in a rush, "I may never see you again. Oh, I wish I could forget you. Go—please, for God's sake, go!"

I held her hand for a moment. She pulled away, but not before pressing something into my palm—the white rose she had held through the entire scene.

While this was happening, the Count was yelling at his servants—swearing, begging, ordering. My conscience later teased me that maybe I'd arranged for them to be drunk and missing when needed. But now they rushed into position, startled and clumsy. The coachmen cracked their whips, and the carriage rolled away into the moonlit street, carrying her toward Paris.

I stood on the sidewalk and watched until it disappeared into the night. Then, with a long sigh, I turned away, the white rose tucked safely in my handkerchief—our secret, something just between us.

Back inside, the innkeeper and his staff had managed to prop up Colonel Gaillarde against the wall using pillows and bags. Someone poured a glass of brandy and tried to give it to him, but even that didn't wake him.

A short, bald military doctor—who once performed nearly ninety amputations after the Battle of Eylau—had retired to this town. He was called in and thought the Colonel might have a fractured skull. At the very least, he had a serious head injury and would need a couple of weeks to recover.

I was starting to feel uneasy. What if this wild night ended with me on trial, or worse—executed? Back then, you never knew whether you'd face a rope or a guillotine.

The Colonel, snoring like a thunderstorm, was taken to his room.

I found the innkeeper in the dining room where we had eaten earlier. When you're trying to win someone over, don't worry about saving money—go big. I ordered his best bottle of wine, made him drink with me (he had two glasses for every one of mine), and handed him thirty-five gold coins as a thank-you for the service.

The moment his fingers touched the money, his cold attitude melted. His face lit up, and he quickly shoved the coins into his pocket with a grateful smile. I could tell he was now firmly on my side.

I brought up the Colonel's condition. We agreed that if I hadn't hit him with my cane, he probably would've killed someone—or several people—right there in the inn. The waiters would back that up in court without hesitation.

Of course, I had another reason to leave as soon as possible: I needed to get to Paris before anything—or anyone—could change.

That's when I got some bad news: no horses were available. The last pair had just been taken by a man staying at our inn, though he had eaten at the Belle Étoile. He was heading to Paris that very night.

Who was he? Had he left yet? Could he be convinced to wait until morning?

The man was upstairs packing. His name was Monsieur Droqville.

I ran upstairs and found my servant, St. Clair, in my room. For a moment, I was distracted.

"St. Clair," I said. "Who is that lady?"

"She's either the Count's daughter or his wife. Doesn't really matter. The same old man you saved from being chopped up by that sword earlier tonight."

"Shut up, idiot. The man's drunk and pretending to be sick—he could talk if he wanted. Now pack up. Which room is Monsieur Droqville's?"

Of course, St. Clair knew. He always did.

Half an hour later, Monsieur Droqville and I were in my carriage, on the road to Paris, using his horses. After a while, I asked him something that had been bothering me.

"Are you sure the lady traveling with the Count is his wife? Doesn't he have a daughter?"

"Yes, I believe she's a very beautiful and charming young woman. She might be his daughter from an earlier marriage, but I can't say for sure. I only saw the Count himself today."

The Marquis was getting sleepy, and before long, he had dozed off in his seat. I nodded off a bit too, but he was out like a light. He only woke briefly at the next post stop, where he'd smartly arranged to have horses ready by sending someone ahead.

"Forgive me for being such a dull travel companion," he said. "I've only had two hours of sleep in the past sixty. I'll grab a cup of coffee now—I've had my nap. You should try one too. Their coffee is excellent."

He ordered two cups of strong black coffee and leaned out the window while waiting. "We'll keep the cups," he said, as he took them and a small tray from the server. "Thank you."

He paid, then passed me a cup. I declined the tray, so he set it on his lap to use as a mini table.

"I hate being rushed," he said. "I like to enjoy my coffee slowly."

I agreed—it really was perfect coffee.

"Like you, Marquis, I haven't had much sleep lately," I said. "This coffee is just what I needed."

The carriage started moving again before we were finished. The coffee kept us talking for a while. The Marquis was smart and easy to talk to, sharing funny and sharp stories about Paris. They were full of useful advice and warnings.

Even though his stories were interesting, I started feeling sleepy again. The Marquis must've noticed, because he let the conversation fade. He tossed his empty cup out the window, did the same with mine, and finally tossed the tray out too. I heard it hit the road behind us—someone walking early in the morning might find it.

I leaned back in my seat with the white rose, now wrapped in white paper, tucked close to my chest. It filled my thoughts with romantic daydreams. I grew drowsier, but I didn't fall asleep. I could still see the inside of the carriage through half-closed eyes.

I wanted to sleep, but I couldn't. Instead, I drifted into a strange, heavy feeling I can't quite describe. The Marquis picked up a dispatch box from the floor, placed it on his knees, and opened it. He pulled out a lamp, hooked it to the window, lit it, and put on his glasses. Then he began to read through a bundle of letters.

We were moving slowly. Earlier, I had insisted on four horses between stops, but now we had only two. The slower speed felt frustrating.

Watching the Marquis quietly read and sort letters became oddly annoying. I wanted to close my eyes and stop looking at him—but I couldn't. I tried again and again, but my eyelids wouldn't move. I even tried to rub my eyes, but nothing happened. My arms wouldn't move. My entire body felt frozen. It was terrifying.

At first, I wasn't even scared. But now I was. Something was wrong—it wasn't just a nightmare. I tried to call out, to make some kind of sound, but I couldn't. I kept trying over and over, but nothing came out.

Meanwhile, the Marquis calmly kept reading. Then he tied up his letters, hummed a tune from an opera, and looked out the window.

"Yes, I see the lights," he said cheerfully. "We'll be there in two or three minutes."

He turned to me, smiled kindly, and gave a little shrug.

"Poor thing," he said. "He must be very tired—fast asleep. He'll wake when the carriage stops."

He put his letters back in the box, locked it, put his glasses away, and looked out again.

We had entered a small town. It must've been after two in the morning. The carriage pulled up to an inn, where a light glowed through the open door.

"Here we are!" he said, smiling as he turned to me. But I didn't move.

"Yes, he must be exhausted," he said, when I didn't respond. Then he spoke to my servant, who had come to the carriage door.

"Your master's sleeping soundly. He's so tired, we shouldn't wake him. Let's go inside while they change the horses. We'll find something for him to eat when he wakes up—he'll be hungry."

He adjusted the lamp, added oil, and smiled again before reminding my servant to let me rest. Then he stepped out and walked toward the inn, chatting casually with St. Clair.

I remained where I was, still frozen, still wide awake—unable to move.

Chapter VIII.
A Three Minutes' Visit

I've felt a lot of physical pain in my life, but nothing as awful as what I experienced then. I hope no one ever has to go through anything like that, not even in death. It was like being trapped in my own body, completely frozen but fully aware. I couldn't move or speak. It was a silent kind of torture.

My mind was working fine. I could hear and see clearly, but I had no control over my body at all. It was like my brain had lost connection with everything else.

The Marquis had left the small lamp burning in the carriage when he went into the inn. I was hoping he'd come back soon and maybe wake me up somehow from this nightmare.

But instead, without any warning or footsteps, the carriage door opened. A stranger climbed in quietly and closed the door behind him.

The lamp gave off a soft light—about the same as a candle—so I could see him clearly. He was a young man wearing a long gray coat with a hood over his head. When he moved, I thought I saw a military cap underneath and could tell by the cuffs of his coat that he was wearing a uniform.

He had a thick mustache and a small beard on his chin. A red scar ran from his upper lip across his cheek.

He sat beside me and leaned in, covering his eyes slightly as he studied my face for a few seconds. He moved like a ghost—quiet and quick, like he had done this kind of thing before. I was sure he was there to rob or even kill me. But I couldn't move a muscle.

He reached into my inside coat pocket and took out everything—my letters and the white rose. Among those papers was one that was very important to me.

He glanced through the letters but clearly wasn't interested in them. He placed them aside along with the rose. Then he focused on one paper and quickly wrote notes in a small notebook.

The way he moved, so fast and quiet, made me think he was probably trained by the police.

When he was done, he put everything back exactly as he'd found it and left, all in less than three minutes.

Not long after that, the Marquis returned. He got back in the carriage and smiled when he looked at me, thinking I was just peacefully asleep. If only he knew the truth.

He picked up where he left off, reading and organizing his letters by the light of the same lamp the stranger had just used.

We were outside the town now, slowly continuing our journey. We'd gone about two leagues when I suddenly felt a strange popping sensation in my ear, like air was rushing into my throat. It was as if a bubble burst inside my head. The tight pressure in my brain suddenly lifted. A weird humming filled my ears, and my whole body began to tingle, like when a numb limb starts to wake up.

I gasped and tried to sit up. I fell back, weak and trembling.

The Marquis turned to me, surprised. "Are you all right?" he asked, taking my hand.

I could only groan.

Slowly, I began to feel better. I was finally able to explain what had happened and told him about the man who had gone through my letters while he was gone.

"My God!" he said. "He didn't touch my dispatch box, did he?"

I told him I didn't think so.

He checked the box carefully and sighed in relief. "Everything's still here, thank heaven. There are letters in here that must never be read by the wrong people."

Then he asked more about what I'd experienced. After listening, he said:

"A friend of mine went through something very similar. It happened on a ship after a very stressful day. He was a brave man, just like you, and had gone through a sudden and intense situation. He thought he had just fallen asleep from exhaustion, but he later described it exactly the way you just did."

"Did it ever happen to him again?" I asked.

"I knew him for years after that, and it never came back," said the Marquis. "It's interesting that both of you had a similar kind of stress before the attack—your fight with that mad colonel, for example, and then lying down to rest."

"I do wonder who that man was who went through your papers," he added. "But it's not worth turning back. We wouldn't find anything. Those people know how to cover their tracks. Still, I'm pretty sure he was from the police. If he were just a thief, he would've stolen something."

I didn't say much after that. I was still shaken and tired. But the Marquis kept the conversation going.

"We're becoming such good friends," he said with a smile. "So I should remind you that, for now, I'm not the Marquis d'Harmonville. I'm traveling under the name Monsieur Droqville. Still, when we reach Paris, I hope I can help you out. I'd like to know what hotel you'll be staying at."

He explained that his real home in Paris, the Hôtel d'Harmonville, was closed except for a few old servants who must not see "Monsieur Droqville." But he promised he'd help me get into the Marquis's opera box and maybe a few other exclusive places.

"And when my secret mission is over," he added, "the real Marquis will insist that you visit him this fall at his château."

I made sure to thank the Marquis.

The closer we got to Paris, the more I appreciated having him by my side. Having someone important looking out for me—especially someone I had met by pure chance—could really turn my trip into something far more exciting and enjoyable than I had expected.

The Marquis was kind and respectful, both in the way he spoke and acted. Just as I was thanking him again, the carriage came to a stop. We had reached the place where fresh horses were waiting for us—and, as it turned out, it was also where we would be saying goodbye.

Chapter IX.
Gossip and Counsel

My long and exciting journey had finally ended. I sat by the window of my hotel, looking out at the bright and busy streets of Paris. In no time at all, the city had come alive again, full of excitement. Everyone had read about how wild things became after Napoleon's fall and the return of the Bourbons. I don't need to go into all the details, especially since it was so long ago, but it really was a strange and exciting time to be there. It was my first visit, and even though I've been back many times since, I don't think I've ever seen Paris quite so alive.

I had been in Paris for two days and had seen many famous sights. Unlike what others had warned me about, I hadn't run into any trouble from the defeated French soldiers, who were supposed to be rude and angry.

But more than anything, my thoughts kept returning to the woman from my adventure. The hope of seeing her again made every walk, carriage ride, and museum visit feel like it had a secret purpose. It made the city feel magical.

Still, I hadn't heard a word from the Count or Countess de St. Alyre, or from the Marquis d'Harmonville. I had fully recovered from the strange illness I experienced during the journey.

It was evening, and I had begun to worry that the Marquis had forgotten me, when the waiter brought up a card that said "Monsieur Droqville." I was thrilled and told him to send the gentleman up right away.

The Marquis entered, just as kind and pleasant as before.

"I've become a bit of a night owl," he said after we exchanged greetings. "I stay out of sight during the day, and even now I barely dared to come here, even in a closed carriage. The people I'm helping think it's very important that no one knows I'm in Paris. But first—here are some tickets for my box at the opera. I'm sorry I can't offer you more for the next couple of weeks. While I was gone, I told my secretary to give it to any of my friends who asked, so now it's nearly all booked."

I thanked him sincerely.

"Now," he said, "let me give you a little friendly advice. You didn't come here without introductions, did you?"

I handed him a few letters of introduction. He glanced at the names and waved them off.

"Don't worry about these," he said. "I'll take you myself to meet the right people. One trusted friend is better than ten letters. But don't rush into socializing yet. You young men usually want to enjoy all the public fun first. So do that—visit all the museums, shows, and places you can. That will keep you busy for at least three weeks. When that's done, I'll be free to introduce you to the more quiet and refined side of Paris. Trust me—once you're in Parisian society, you stay in."

I promised to follow his advice, and he seemed pleased.

He then helped me make a list of must-see places using my city map. He added all kinds of funny and interesting stories about each one as we went.

"In a week or two," he said, "I'll be free to help you more. But until then, be careful. Don't gamble—if you do, you'll be robbed. This city is full of charming crooks just waiting to take advantage of strangers. Only trust people you know."

Again, I thanked him and said I'd be careful. But I couldn't stop myself from asking about the lady I'd helped at the inn. I wanted to know more about the Count and Countess de St. Alyre.

Sadly, he hadn't seen them since that night. He didn't know where they were staying. They owned an old house a few miles from Paris, but he thought they might still be in the city for a few more days, getting ready to return home after being away for so long.

"How long have they been gone?" I asked.

"About eight months."

"They're not wealthy, right?"

"Not by your standards," he said. "But they live comfortably and quietly in the countryside."

"So they must be happy?"

"You'd think so."

"But they're not?"

"The Count is very jealous."

"But surely his wife hasn't given him any reason?"

"I think she has."

"How?"

"Well," he said, hesitating. "She's a little too... a lot too..."

"Too what?"

"Too beautiful. But even with her amazing eyes, perfect features, and flawless skin, I believe she's an honest woman. You've never seen her?"

"There was a woman at the inn," I said carefully. "She was wrapped in a cloak and wearing a thick veil. I couldn't see her face."

"She might have been his daughter. Do they argue?"

"You mean the Count and his wife?"

"Yes."

"A little."

"What about?"

"It's a long story. About her diamonds. They're worth about a million francs. The Count wants her to sell them and use the money for income, however she wants. But she refuses, and I think she has a reason she hasn't told him."

"What reason?"

"She's saving them for when she marries her second husband," he said with a sly smile.

"Oh? But the Count's a good man, isn't he?"

"Very good—and smart too."

"I'd really like to meet him. You said he's..."

"So happily married? Yes. But they live quietly. He might take her to the opera now and then, but that's it."

"He must remember so much about the old times and the revolution."

"Yes, he's the perfect person for a thinker like you. He naps after dinner. His wife doesn't. But seriously, they've stepped away from public life. He's become uninterested in everything—and so has she. Not even her husband seems to catch her attention anymore."

The Marquis stood up to leave.

"Don't spend your money gambling," he said. "You'll soon have a better chance to spend it wisely. Several amazing art collections are going to be sold soon. You could get some amazing deals! I'll let you know when. Oh—and I nearly forgot! Next week there's going to be a big masquerade ball at Versailles—more grand than usual. Everyone wants tickets. But I think I can get one for you. Good night! Farewell!"

Chapter X.
The Black Veil

Speaking French fluently and having plenty of money meant I could enjoy everything Paris had to offer. You can probably imagine how I spent those two days—busy and full of excitement. At about the same hour as before, Monsieur Droqville returned for another visit.

He was as friendly and cheerful as ever. He told me that the masquerade ball was set for the following Wednesday and that he had already gotten me a ticket.

I was really disappointed because I was afraid I wouldn't be able to go.

He gave me a sharp look that I didn't understand and asked a little harshly, "And why not, Monsieur Beckett?"

His tone surprised me. I answered honestly—I had made plans for that evening with a few English friends and didn't know how I could get out of it.

"Exactly!" he snapped. "You English always run straight to your fellow countrymen, to your beer and steak. Instead of getting to know the people and culture here, you just sit around drinking, smoking, and swearing with each other. You leave without learning anything!"

He gave a sarcastic laugh and looked like he could've poisoned me.

"There," he said, tossing the card onto the table. "Take it or leave it. I suppose I went through all this trouble for nothing. But normally, when someone like me does a favor for someone, it's not returned with rudeness."

I was shocked. His reaction felt very rude to me, but I realized I might have unknowingly offended him according to French manners. I felt a mix of embarrassment, guilt, and regret. I rushed to apologize and thank him properly for his help.

I told him I would cancel my other plans no matter what, that I had spoken carelessly, and that I hadn't thanked him enough for his kindness.

"Say no more," he replied, softening. "I was only upset because I didn't want you to miss something so special. I may have spoken too strongly, but I hope you'll forgive me. People who know me well know I sometimes say more than I should—and I always regret it. Please forget that I lost my temper for a moment. Let's stay good friends."

He smiled warmly, like the same kind man I'd first met at the Belle Étoile, and held out his hand. I shook it respectfully and gladly. Our little disagreement seemed to have made our friendship stronger.

The Marquis then told me I should try to book a hotel room in Versailles right away because the place would be packed. He suggested going the next morning to make sure I got one.

I ordered horses for 11 a.m., and after chatting a bit more, he wished me good night, held a handkerchief to his face as he hurried down the stairs, and jumped into his closed carriage. I watched from the window as he drove off.

The next day I arrived in Versailles. As I neared the Hotel de France, it was clear I had cut it close—maybe too close. The entrance was surrounded by carriages, so many that I had to get down and squeeze between horses just to get inside. The lobby was packed with guests and servants all yelling at the hotel owner, who was trying to explain, politely but desperately, that not a single room or even a closet was free.

I quickly stepped back outside, leaving them to keep arguing in vain. I got into my carriage and told my driver to go as fast as possible to the Hotel du Reservoir. But it was the same situation there—carriages everywhere, the place totally full.

It was frustrating, but what could I do? My postilion had, a bit too eagerly, nudged our way slowly through the crowd while I was inside talking to the hotel manager. Now we were right in front of the door, which was convenient for getting back into the carriage. But that was where the good news ended—there were still carriages blocking us in from the front, the back, and even in rows on both sides.

At that time, my eyesight was incredibly sharp. If I had been a little impatient before, imagine how I felt when I saw an open carriage pass along a narrow path across the road. I was certain I recognized the veiled Countess and her husband inside. The carriage had to slow down because a cart ahead was taking up the whole space and moving at a crawl, as usual.

I should've done the smart thing and gotten out onto the sidewalk, walked around the row of carriages, and met the barouche from the front. But instead, I acted without thinking, more like a soldier charging ahead than a strategist. I leaped over the back seat of the carriage next to mine—don't ask me how—tumbled through a small buggy where an old man and his dog were napping, stepped over the side of another open carriage where four men were loudly arguing, tripped as I got out the other side, and fell face-first across a pair of horses. They panicked, started kicking, and threw me to the ground, right into the dust.

To anyone watching, who didn't know what I was trying to do, I must've looked completely out of my mind. Luckily, the Countess's carriage had already passed by the time I hit the ground. Covered in dust, with my hat crushed, I knew I couldn't possibly show myself to her in that condition.

I stood up in the middle of a chorus of angry yelling—mixed with laughter—and started brushing myself off. Just then, I heard a familiar voice call out, "Monsieur Beckett."

It was the Marquis, leaning out of a nearby carriage window. I was so relieved to see him that I quickly made my way over.

"You might as well leave Versailles," he said. "I'm sure you've already found out that there's not a single room left in either hotel—and I can add that there's not a single available room in the whole town. But I've made arrangements for you somewhere just as good. Tell your servant to follow us, and hop in."

Just then, a gap opened up in the line of carriages, and mine pulled up. I told my servant to follow, then jumped into the Marquis's carriage. As soon as the Marquis gave his driver instructions, we started moving.

"I'm taking you to a comfortable little place that hardly anyone in Paris knows about. Since I already knew what the situation would be here, I reserved a room for you. It's only about a mile away, in an old inn called the Flying Dragon. Lucky for you, my business brought me here early."

We drove about a mile and a half to the far side of the palace, down a narrow, old road. On one side were the woods of Versailles, and on the other stood giant, ancient trees—larger than what you usually see in France.

We stopped in front of a solid old inn made of stone, decorated more grandly than most buildings of its kind. It looked like it had once been a wealthy person's home. Carved coats of arms and decorative symbols along the walls suggested that the original owner had been someone important. A newer porch stuck out from the front, with a wide arch above it. Carved and painted on the stone arch was a colorful Flying Dragon—red and gold wings stretched out, a green and gold tail curled in loops, ending in a sharp, golden tip like a deadly dart.

"I won't go in," said the Marquis, "but you'll find it comfortable. It's certainly better than nothing. I'd join you, but I'm keeping a low profile right now. You'll probably be pleased to know the inn is haunted—or at least I would have been when I was younger. Just don't mention that to the innkeeper—it's a touchy subject."

He gave me a sly smile. "If you want to enjoy the ball tonight, wear a domino. I'll probably be there too, in the same kind of costume. But how shall we recognize each other? A flower won't work—too many people wear them. How about this: you wear a red cross, about two inches long, pinned to your costume, and I'll wear a white one. And wherever you go, stay near the door until we find each other. I'll check every door I pass, and you do the same. We'll meet soon enough."

Then he added, "I can't enjoy these things unless I'm with someone young—someone who still finds joy in everything. Farewell. See you tonight."

By this time, I had stepped out of the carriage. I closed the door, wished him goodbye, and watched as he rode off.

Chapter XI.
The Dragon Volant

I glanced around, taking in the view.

The building had a lot of character, and the tall trees surrounding it made the whole scene even more striking. The peaceful, old-time vibe was completely different from the bright, noisy streets of Paris I had just come from.

I spent a minute looking at the colorful old sign above the door. Then I took a better look at the house itself. It was large and solid, and it reminded me more of an old English inn—the kind you imagine travelers staying at during the time of the Canterbury tales—than a typical French inn. The only thing that gave away its French style was a round tower on the left side, topped with a pointed roof like a little castle.

I walked in and introduced myself as Monsieur Beckett, the guest with the reserved room. Right away, they treated me like an important visitor—like I was some rich English nobleman with endless money.

The innkeeper showed me to my room. It was big and a little dark, with wood paneling and old-fashioned furniture that looked like it hadn't been updated in a hundred years. The fireplace was wide, and the heavy mantel above it was carved with symbols that probably matched the ones I saw on the outside of the building. The whole room had a kind of quiet sadness to it, like it held onto memories. I went to the window and looked out.

Behind the building was a small park, and beyond that, a thick forest. In the middle of it stood a château with tall pointed towers— just like the one attached to the inn. The château looked lonely and a bit forgotten. It had clearly been neglected. The whole scene gave off a quiet, sad feeling.

"What's that château called?" I asked the innkeeper.

"That, Monsieur, is the Château de la Carque," he replied.

"It's a shame it's been left like that," I said. "Maybe the owner doesn't have enough money to fix it up?"

"Maybe," he said.

"Maybe?" I asked again, watching him closely. "So people don't really like him around here?"

"Not really liked or disliked," he answered. "I just meant that even if he had money, no one knows what he'd use it for."

"And who owns it?" I asked.

"The Count de St. Alyre."

"The Count?" I repeated, more alert now. "Are you sure?"

"Very sure, Monsieur. The Count de St. Alyre."

"Does he live here often?"

"Not much. He's away for long stretches," the innkeeper said.

"Is he poor?"

"I rent this place from him. The rent isn't high, but he always needs it quickly," he replied with a small, sarcastic smile.

"But I've heard he's not really poor," I said.

"People say he gambles. Who really knows? What I do know is that he never keeps his money long. A few months ago, a relative of his died far away. They brought the body here and buried it in Père Lachaise, like the man had asked. The Count seemed really upset—though they say he got a good amount of money from that death. Still, the money never seems to last."

"He's old, right?"

"Old? Around here we call him the 'Wandering Jew'—except he's not always got even a few coins on him. But still, he had the nerve to marry a young and beautiful wife."

"And she?" I asked, hoping to hear more.

"She's the Countess de St. Alyre."

"Yes, but what else is there to say about her?"

"Three things," he said. "She's young, she's beautiful, and she has diamonds."

I laughed. He was clearly dodging my question on purpose.

"I see," I said. "You don't want to—"

"Start any problems with the Count," he finished. "Exactly. He could cause trouble for me, and I could cause trouble for him. But it's easier if we both mind our own business. You get what I mean."

So I gave up for now. Maybe he really didn't know anything else. Or maybe he was just waiting for me to offer a bribe. I could always try that later if I felt like he was hiding something.

The innkeeper was an older man, skinny, sun-tanned, and sharp-eyed, with the confident attitude of someone who'd spent years in the military. I found out later he had served under Napoleon during the Italian campaigns.

"I think there's one question you can answer without any risk," I said. "Is the Count home right now?"

"He has many homes, I think," the innkeeper said, a little carefully. "But yes, I believe he's staying at the Château de la Carque at the moment."

I looked out the window again, now more curious than ever.

"I saw him today, in a carriage at Versailles," I said.

"Not surprising," he answered.

"Then I guess his carriage, horses, and servants are at the château?"

"He keeps the carriage here. The servants are just hired for the trip. Only one of them stays overnight at the château. It must be a scary life for the Countess," he added.

"The old miser!" I thought. "He's probably putting pressure on her to give up her diamonds. What a miserable life—stuck between jealousy and control."

I sighed and looked again at the tall towers of the château, framed by those dark trees. What a mess. And honestly, don't we all make fools of ourselves at some point? We don't really get wiser as we grow up— we just chase different dreams.

At that moment, my servant St. Clair walked in and started unpacking my things.

"Did you get a bed?" I asked.

"In the attic, Monsieur—sharing space with spiders, and I swear, cats and owls too. But we're getting along just fine. Long live the little things!"

"I didn't realize it would be this crowded," I said.

"Mostly the servants, Monsieur, of the people lucky enough to get rooms in Versailles."

"And what do you think of the Dragon Volant?"

"The Dragon Volant! Monsieur—the fiery dragon! If people are telling the truth, it's as bad as the devil himself! I swear on my Christian faith, they say strange and creepy things have happened in this house."

"What do you mean? Ghosts?"

"No, sir, I wish it were only ghosts. That would be better. Not ghosts—these are people who disappeared—right in front of witnesses—gone without a trace."

"What are you saying, St. Clair? Tell me the story—or miracle—or whatever it is."

"It's simple, Monsieur. There was once a former master of the royal stables—he worked for the late king before the Revolution. He was allowed to return to France under the Emperor and stayed in this very hotel for a month. At the end of that time, he vanished—right in front of several trustworthy people who saw the whole thing. Just disappeared!

"There was another case too—a tall Russian nobleman, over six feet. He was standing downstairs in the main room, telling seven reliable men about the last moments of Peter the Great. He had a glass of brandy in one hand and a nearly empty cup of coffee in the other— and just like that, he vanished too. They found his boots on the floor where he'd been standing. The man to his right suddenly found the Russian's coffee cup in his hand. The man to his left was holding his glass of brandy—"

"Which he probably drank in shock," I joked.

"No, Monsieur—it was saved as a curious item for three years! The village priest accidentally broke it during a chat with Mademoiselle Fidone in the housekeeper's room. But the Russian nobleman? No one ever saw or heard from him again. I tell you, Monsieur, when I leave the Dragon Volant, I hope it's through the front door! I heard all this from the driver who brought us here."

"Well then, it must be true!" I said with a laugh, trying to make light of it. But deep down, I was starting to feel the heaviness of this place— the strange mood of the room, the dark view outside. I couldn't explain it, but I felt a chill, like something bad might happen. My joke came out forced, and I couldn't shake the uneasy feeling.

Chapter XII.

The Magician

There could be no more amazing sight than this masked ball. One of the grand halls open that night was the huge Gallery of Mirrors, lit with four thousand wax candles. The lights reflected endlessly in the mirrors, making the whole place shine so brightly it almost hurt to look. Every room was full of people in colorful costumes, music played everywhere, and the air buzzed with laughter, jokes, and dancing. I had never seen anything as exciting or beautiful in my life.

Wearing my mask and domino costume, I strolled slowly through the rooms. Sometimes I paused to enjoy a funny song, a clever joke, or a little skit. But I also kept an eye out for my friend in the black domino with a white cross on his chest, just like we had agreed.

I had been looking carefully at every doorway as I passed, but I still hadn't seen him.

As I stood watching, enjoying the fun, I saw a fancy, gold-decorated sedan chair—or more like a Chinese-style palanquin—carried by four men in bright costumes. One man led the way with a wand, another followed behind, and beside it walked a serious-looking man in a tall hat, like a dervish, with a long black beard. His robe was covered in symbols, stitched in gold and black thread. His shoes were curved at the toes like something from the East, and he carried a strange book under one arm and a black wand in the other. His face was dark and serious, and he stared at the floor as he walked.

The group stopped near where I stood. The carriers and wand-bearers clapped their hands and danced around the palanquin in a strange but well-practiced way. As they danced, they clapped and chanted together.

Just then, someone touched my arm. I turned and saw a black domino with a white cross—it was the Marquis.

"I'm so glad I found you," he said. "And at the perfect moment. This group is the best in the room. You have to speak to the magician. I met them earlier and asked a few questions. I couldn't believe the answers. Even though he spoke in riddles, it was obvious he knew things only I and a few others could possibly know. I saw others get just as shocked—and even more scared."

He nodded toward a thin figure nearby. It was the Count.

"Come," he said, "I'll introduce you."

Of course, I followed him eagerly.

The Marquis introduced me with a polite comment about how I had helped him during the trouble at the Belle Étoile. The Count thanked me politely too, and said something I liked even more:

"The Countess is in the next room, talking with her old friend the Duchess d'Argensaque. I'll bring her over in a moment to meet you— and to thank you herself for your brave help that night."

"You have to talk to the magician," said the Marquis to the Count. "You'll love it. I did—and his answers were amazing! I still don't know what to make of it."

"Really? Then let's try," the Count replied.

We walked together toward the palanquin, where the serious man with the beard stood. A young man in a Spanish costume, who had just asked his own questions, walked past us and said to his friend,

"Amazing trick! Who's inside that thing? He seems to know everything about everyone!"

The Count moved stiffly with us toward the magician. The Chinese helpers kept a circle clear around the palanquin, and a crowd of onlookers stood around watching.

One of the wand-carriers came forward and held out his hand.

"Money?" the Count asked.

"Gold," the man replied.

The Count gave him a gold coin, and so did the Marquis and I.

The magician stood by the palanquin, holding its curtain with one hand and leaning on his wand with the other. His head was bowed, his eyes on the ground. He looked like a statue—completely still. He didn't speak. When the Count asked, "Am I married or unmarried?" the magician pulled back the curtain, leaned in to listen to the person inside, then closed the curtain and said, "Yes."

Every question worked this way. The magician acted like he was just the messenger, repeating what the person in the palanquin said.

The Count asked a few more questions. The Marquis laughed at the answers, but I didn't understand them—probably inside jokes about the Count's life.

"Does my wife love me?" the Count asked playfully.

"As much as you deserve," came the answer.

"Who do I love most in the world?"

"Yourself."

"Well, I suppose that's true for most people. But if we ignore myself, is there anything I love more than my wife?"

"Her diamonds."

The Count gave a short, annoyed reply. The Marquis chuckled.

The Count then asked more seriously, "Is it true there's been a battle in Naples?"

"No, in France."

"Really?" said the Count, clearly annoyed. "Between who?"

"Between the Count and Countess de St. Alyre, over a document they signed on July 25th, 1811."

Later, the Marquis told me that was the date of their marriage contract.

The Count stood frozen. I imagined he was blushing under his mask. Only the Marquis and I knew who he really was.

I think he was about to give up and stop asking questions—he seemed embarrassed. But then the Marquis whispered to him, "Look to your right. See who's coming."

I looked where he pointed and saw a tall, grim-looking man walking toward us. He wasn't wearing a mask. His face was wide, pale, and scarred.

It was Colonel Gaillarde. He was dressed as a soldier from the Imperial Guard, with one arm made to look like a stump and his coat sleeve pinned up. There were real bandages on his eyebrow and temple—left by my walking stick. Another set of scars for his collection.

Chapter XIII.
The Oracle Tells Me Wonders

For a moment, I forgot that my mask and costume completely hid my identity from the old soldier's intense stare, and I almost got ready for a fight. It only lasted a second, of course, but I noticed the Count quietly step back as Colonel Gaillarde, dressed up as a loud, boastful corporal in a blue uniform with white vest and gaiters, marched toward us. He was just as obnoxious in costume as he was in real life as a colonel of dragoons. Twice already, he had almost been kicked out of the party for loudly praising Napoleon in a ridiculous, over-the-top way and had nearly gotten into a fight with a Prussian soldier. In fact, he would've been in several serious fights that night if he hadn't remembered his real goal—trying to win the heart of a rich widow who, he thought, had shown some interest in him. Getting thrown out by the police wouldn't have helped his chances.

"Money? Gold? Bah!" he shouted. "What money can a wounded soldier like me have? I've only got one good hand, and it's holding my sword—it can't go grabbing loot from a defeated enemy!"

"No gold from him," said the magician calmly. "His scars are enough."

"Bravo, prophet! Well said!" the colonel bellowed. "Here I am. Shall I begin asking my questions, oh wise one?"

Without waiting for permission, he launched into his questions in a booming voice. After five or six, he asked, "Who am I chasing right now?"

"Two people," the magician answered.

"Two? Who are they?"

"An Englishman. If you catch him, he'll kill you. And a French widow. If you find her, she'll spit in your face."

"The prophet tells it like it is and hides behind his costume," Gaillarde sneered. "Fine! Why am I chasing them?"

"The widow broke your heart. The Englishman cracked your skull. Each of them is stronger than you on their own—if you're not careful, chasing them might push them together."

"Bah! How could that happen?"

"The Englishman protects women. That idea is stuck in your head. If the widow sees him doing that, she'll marry him. He's young, and becoming a colonel takes time."

"I'll teach him a lesson," the colonel muttered with a grin. Then he asked in a softer tone, "Where is she?"

"Close enough to be insulted if you fail."

"As she should be! You're right, prophet! A hundred thanks. Goodbye!" With that, he stretched his neck to scan the crowd and walked off proudly in his flashy costume, scars, and bearskin hat.

All the while, I had been trying to get a good look at the person sitting inside the palanquin. I only had one clear moment to peek, but what I saw was strange. The person inside was dressed richly in Chinese-style clothes and was much larger than the magician who stood outside. His face looked big and heavy, and his head was tilted forward with his chin resting on his chest. His eyes were shut, and he didn't move at all—he looked lifeless, like a statue. The red glow on his skin seemed to come from the red silk curtains around him. The stillness of his face was even more intense than the quiet man standing outside the palanquin. I only had a few seconds to observe, but it left a strong impression.

The path was clear now, and the Marquis said, "Go ahead, my friend."

So I stepped forward. As I approached the magician with the black wand, I glanced behind me to check if the Count was nearby. He wasn't—he and the Marquis were several steps back, talking about something else entirely. That gave me some relief. The magician had a habit of blurting out secrets, and I wasn't sure the Count would be happy to hear mine.

I paused to think for a second. I decided to test the prophet. After all, it wasn't common to find someone from the Church of England in Paris.

"What is my religion?" I asked.

"A beautiful heresy," the oracle answered right away.

"A heresy?" I said. "And what's it called?"

"Love."

"Oh, then I guess I'm a polytheist—I love many?"

"One," he replied.

Trying to change the subject, I asked, "Have I ever memorized any prayers?"

"Yes."

"Can you repeat one?"

"Come closer."

I leaned in. The magician closed the curtain and whispered clearly:

"I might never see you again—and oh, how I wish I could forget you! Please go—goodbye—for heaven's sake, just go!"

I jumped. These were the exact words the Countess had whispered to me. No one else could have possibly heard them—until now.

I stared at the magician's face. It showed no emotion at all, like he had no idea what those words meant to me.

"What do I want most?" I asked, barely thinking.

"Paradise."

"And what keeps me from getting there?"

"A black veil."

The answers were getting more and more specific. It was like this magician knew every tiny detail of my secret romance—things not even the Marquis could have known! And I was wearing a full disguise—cloak, mask, everything. Even my own brother wouldn't have recognized me.

"You said I loved someone. Does she love me back?" I asked.

"Try."

I lowered my voice even more and stepped closer to the man with the beard so he wouldn't have to answer loudly.

"Does anyone love me?" I repeated.

"Secretly," he said.

"How much?" I asked.

"More than she should."

"How long will that love last?"

"Until the rose drops its petals."

Another clue, tied to the rose! My heart sank.

"Then comes the darkness," I whispered. "But until then, I live in the light."

"The light of violet eyes."

Love—whether or not it's a religion like the magician said—can definitely feel like one. It lifts your imagination, weakens your logic, and makes you believe anything.

If someone else had told me this story, I would've laughed. But when it was happening to me, it overwhelmed me. It made me want her even more. It messed with my thoughts. It even pushed me to act on impulse.

The magician waved me away with his black wand. As I stepped back, still watching the scene in front of me, it all felt even more mysterious and magical now. I moved carefully toward the crowd again. Just then, the magician lifted his arm quickly in a commanding gesture. It was a signal to the man with the golden wand.

That man hit his wand against the ground and called out in a sharp voice, "The great Confu is silent for an hour."

Right away, the bearers dropped a bamboo screen down in front of the palanquin with a loud snap, locking it in place. Then the magician—the one in the tall fez, with the long black beard and wand—began a strange, slow dance, like a dervish. The gold-wand men joined him. The bearers joined too, dancing in wide circles around the palanquin.

The movements started slow, calm, and serious. Then, bit by bit, they got faster. Their motions grew sharper and wilder until the dancers were spinning like they were caught in a storm. They moved so fast they blurred, like a wheel spinning at full speed. The crowd clapped in amazement.

And just like that, the dancers scattered and blended into the crowd. The show—at least for now—was over.

I saw the Marquis d'Harmonville nearby, standing quietly and looking down, lost in thought. I walked over to him.

"The Count just left to find his wife," he said. "Too bad she didn't get to ask the magician something. That would've been entertaining—especially watching the Count's reaction. Let's go after him. I asked him to introduce you."

My heart started pounding as I followed the Marquis d'Harmonville.

Chapter XIV.
Mademoiselle De La Vallière

We walked together through the crowded rooms, the Marquis and I, searching for the Count. It wasn't easy to spot anyone in the packed space.

"Wait here," said the Marquis. "I just thought of a better way to find him. Besides, he might be feeling jealous and think there's no benefit in introducing you to his wife. I'll go and talk to him. You seem very eager to meet her."

We were in the room now known as the Salon d'Apollon. I remember the paintings clearly, and as it turned out, something unforgettable would happen to me in that very room.

I sat down on a large, golden sofa. There were three or four other people sitting there, chatting happily. Everyone except the woman seated next to me. She was very close—less than two feet away—and completely silent, lost in thought. Her posture was graceful and still. She wore a costume like the one in Collignan's portrait of Mademoiselle de la Vallière—elegant and richly detailed. Her powdered hair had a dark brown tone underneath, and I noticed one perfectly shaped foot and a very beautiful hand.

But she still wore her mask, unlike many others who had taken theirs off. I was sure she was beautiful. Taking advantage of the masquerade's mystery, where nobody knows anyone unless they speak or drop a hint, I said something:

"It's not easy to fool me, Mademoiselle."

"Good for you, Monsieur," she replied calmly.

"I mean," I continued, pretending to recognize her, "that beauty is harder to hide than you might think."

"And yet you've hidden yours quite well," she answered with the same sweet and casual tone.

"I see you dressed as the famous Mademoiselle de la Vallière, and I think you're even more graceful than she was. I look at your mask and still recognize you. Beauty is like that magic stone from the Arabian Nights—it glows, even when it's hidden."

"I know that story," she said. "But the stone only glowed in the dark. Aren't these rooms filled with light? I thought we were in the glow that follows a certain Countess wherever she goes?"

That comment threw me off. Was she teasing me? Could she be friends with the Countess? Or just stirring trouble? I had to be careful.

"What Countess?" I asked.

"If you really know me, you know who my best friend is. Isn't she beautiful?"

"There are so many Countesses…" I answered vaguely.

"Everyone who knows me knows who I'm closest to. So you don't know me?"

"That's harsh. I still believe I'm not mistaken."

"Who were you walking with earlier?" she asked.

"A gentleman. A friend," I replied.

"I saw him. I think I know who he is. Isn't he a certain Marquis?"

Now I was stuck again. Another question I couldn't answer honestly.

"There are so many people here, and sometimes you walk with one person, and later with another—"

"Which makes it easy for a dishonest man to avoid a simple question. But I'll still treat you with respect, since you're being cautious."

"Mademoiselle would think less of me if I shared someone else's secrets."

"But you haven't fooled me. You're just copying your friend's secretive style. I hate that. It means you're hiding something or too scared to say the truth. Do you think I don't know who he is? The man with the little white cross on his chest? I know the Marquis d'Harmonville very well. So much for your clever cover story."

"I can't confirm or deny your guess."

"You don't need to. But why would you insult a lady like this?"

"That's the last thing I wanted to do."

"You acted like you knew me—but you don't. You wanted to chat, not with a person, but with a pretty costume. You thought I looked good, so you made a guess and hoped to have fun talking to someone you don't even know. But no one is perfect. Has honesty disappeared from the world?"

"Mademoiselle, you're mistaken about me."

"And you've misjudged me too. I'm not as simple as you thought. I know exactly who you're hoping to charm with your sad compliments—and I know who you've been trying to find all night."

"Then tell me who you think that is," I said.

"I will, on one condition."

"What is it?"

"That you'll admit I'm right if I guess correctly."

"That's not fair. You're twisting my intentions. I never said I came here to flatter anyone in that way."

"I won't press you on that. But if I guess the right lady, you'll have to admit it."

"Do I really have to promise?"

"Of course not—but if you don't, I won't say another word to you."

I hesitated. But how could she possibly know? The Countess wouldn't have told anyone about our moment. And this masked lady couldn't possibly know who I was.

"Fine," I said. "I promise."

"Swear it on your honor as a gentleman."

"I do, on my honor as a gentleman."

"Then the lady you're hoping to meet is the Countess de St. Alyre."

I was shocked. I didn't know what to say. But I had made a promise, so I answered:

"Yes, the Countess de St. Alyre is the lady I hoped to be introduced to tonight. But I swear, also on my honor, that she has no idea I was hoping for that. In fact, she probably doesn't even remember that I exist. I once did her and the Count a small favor—too small, I'm afraid, to be remembered for more than an hour."

"The world isn't as ungrateful as you think. And even if most people are, there are a few who aren't. I can tell you that the Countess de St. Alyre never forgets a kindness. She may not show it, but that's because she's unhappy—she simply can't."

"Unhappy? I was afraid that might be true. But as for the rest of what you're saying, it sounds more like a pleasant fantasy."

"I told you I'm her friend, didn't I? That means I know what kind of person she is. She's also confided in me. So maybe I know more than you think about that little favor you're so quick to dismiss."

I was growing more and more curious—and, if I'm honest, more tempted. I wasn't any better than most young men, and now that my pride and feelings were involved, the right and wrong of the situation seemed to matter a lot less. My thoughts were back on the Countess— her image pushed everything else out of my mind. I would have given anything just to hear that she remembered me—that she hadn't forgotten the man who stood up for her, facing down an angry soldier with nothing but a wooden stick.

"You said she's unhappy," I said. "What's making her life so hard?"

"A lot of things. Her husband is old, jealous, and controlling. Isn't that reason enough? And even when he's not around, she's still alone."

"But I thought you were her friend?"

"And do you think one friend is enough?" she asked. "She only has one person she can really talk to."

"Is there room for one more friend?"

"Try."

"But how can I even begin?"

"She'll help you."

"How?"

She replied with a question of her own. "Did you get a room at either of the hotels in Versailles?"

"No, I couldn't. I'm staying at the Dragon Volant. It's right at the edge of the Château de la Carque's grounds."

"Even better. I don't need to ask if you're brave enough for an adventure. I don't need to ask if you're honorable. I know a lady can trust you and be safe. There aren't many men who could be given this chance without causing harm. You'll meet her at two o'clock in the morning, in the park of the Château de la Carque. What room are you staying in at the Dragon Volant?"

I was stunned by how bold and confident she was. Was she playing a trick on me?

"I can describe it," I said. "If you look out the back of the inn, my room is at the far right corner, one floor up from the ground."

"Good. If you looked out toward the park, you might have seen a few thick clusters of chestnut and lime trees. They're grouped close together like a small grove. Go back to your room now, change your clothes, and don't tell anyone where you're going or why. Leave the Dragon Volant quietly, climb the park wall without being seen, and find the grove I mentioned. The Countess will meet you there. She'll only speak with you for a few minutes, but during that time, she'll explain things I couldn't tell you here."

I can't really explain how I felt when I heard those words. I was shocked. Then I started to doubt them. I couldn't believe something so exciting could actually be true.

"Mademoiselle, if I could be sure that this incredible honor is truly meant for me, I would be grateful for the rest of my life. But how can I be sure you're not just being kind or thoughtful, rather than certain that the Countess de St. Alyre truly wants this?"

"Monsieur, you must think either I'm not really in on the secret you believed was only shared between you and the Countess—or worse, that I'm playing a cruel joke. But I swear I am in her confidence. I swear it on everything dear, including the last whisper of a goodbye." She gently touched a white rosebud in her bouquet. "I swear it by my good luck, and hers—or maybe I should say our lucky star. Isn't that enough?"

"Enough?" I repeated. "More than enough—thank you a thousand times."

"So if I know her secret, I must be her friend. And if I'm her friend, why would I use her name just to pull a cheap trick on a stranger like you?"

"Please forgive me for doubting. You have to understand how much it means to me just to have a chance to see and speak with the Countess. Is it really so strange that I hesitated to believe it? But you've convinced me, and I hope you'll forgive me."

"You'll be at the place I described, then, at two o'clock?"

"Definitely," I said.

"And I know you're not someone who's afraid of a little danger. No need to say it—I already know your courage."

"In this case, I welcome any danger."

"Then maybe you should go now, Monsieur, and find your friend again?"

"He asked me to wait here. The Count de St. Alyre said he would bring me to meet the Countess."

"And you actually believe him?" she asked with a light laugh.

"Why shouldn't I?"

"Because he's jealous and clever. Just watch—he'll come back and say he couldn't find her, or she moved, or something. He'll promise to do it another time."

"I think I see him now, walking toward us with my friend. But... no, the Countess isn't with him."

"I told you so. If you're waiting to meet her through him, it's going to be a long wait. You'd better step away now. If he sees us talking, he'll guess we were speaking about his wife—and that will make him even more jealous and watchful."

I thanked the mysterious masked lady and stepped back a few paces. I circled around a little so I could meet the Count from the side, acting as if I'd just wandered over. I smiled to myself under my mask when he told me that the Duchess de la Roqueme had changed seats and taken the Countess with her—but that he hoped to introduce me another time.

I made sure to avoid the Marquis d'Harmonville, who was following the Count. I was worried he'd try to walk back with me, and I didn't want to have to explain anything.

So I quickly slipped into the crowd and made my way toward the Hall of Mirrors, heading in the opposite direction of the Count and the Marquis.

Chapter XV.
Strange Story of the Dragon Volant

These parties used to start earlier back then, especially in France, compared to the balls in modern-day London. I checked my watch— it was just after midnight.

The night was hot and still. Even though the rooms were huge, they felt stuffy because of all the people, the masks, and the hundreds of lights adding to the heat. Like some others, I took off my mask to breathe easier. I had just done that when I heard someone call my name—it was a friendly English voice.

It was Tom Whistlewick from the —th Dragoons. His face was red, and like me, he had taken off his mask. He was one of those newly famous Waterloo officers, admired by everyone except the French. The only fault I knew of his was that he had a habit of drinking a bit too much champagne at events like this.

Tom introduced me to his friend, Monsieur Carmaignac. He was a small, thin man who stood perfectly straight, bald, wore glasses, and took snuff. I soon found out he worked for the government.

Tom was in a cheerful, talkative mood—almost too cheerful to understand—but after some light conversation, he settled down quietly, fanning himself with his mask. He slowly sat on a bench beside us and seemed to be struggling to keep his eyes open.

"I heard you mention," said Monsieur Carmaignac, "that you're staying at the Dragon Volant—about half a mile from here. When I worked in a different police office four years ago, two very strange cases happened there. One was a wealthy Frenchman, allowed back into France by the Emperor—he disappeared. The other was a Russian nobleman. He vanished too, just as mysteriously."

"My servant told me something confusing about that," I said. "He mentioned the same people—a returning French noble and a Russian. But he made it sound so supernatural that I didn't believe a word of it."

"No, there was nothing supernatural," the Frenchman said. "But it was definitely strange. No one ever figured it out."

"I'd like to hear the story," I said. "Especially since I'm staying there. You don't suspect the current owners, do you?"

"Oh no, the place has changed hands since then. But there seemed to be something unlucky about a certain room."

"Can you describe the room?"

"Of course. It's a large, wood-paneled bedroom, up one flight of stairs, at the far right when you look out the back windows."

"Really?" I said, now more curious—and a little uneasy. "That's exactly the room I have!"

"Did the people die, or were they just... gone?"

"They disappeared in very strange ways," he replied. "I'll tell you the details. I know them exactly because I visited the house myself during the first case to gather information. For the second case, I didn't go personally, but I saw the reports and wrote the official letter to the missing man's family. They had asked the government to investigate. We got a letter from the family more than two years later saying the man had still not turned up."

He took a pinch of snuff and looked straight at me.

"Never seen again. I'll tell you everything we knew. The Frenchman was Chevalier Chateau Blassemare. Unlike most nobles who fled, he acted early, sold a lot of property before the revolution got too bad, and left with a large sum of money. He brought about half a million francs with him to France, most of which he invested in the national funds. He also had money in Austria. So he was rich and not in debt."

I nodded.

"He didn't live extravagantly. He had a nice place in Paris and enjoyed the theater and society, but he didn't gamble. He was middle-aged, tried to seem younger than he was, and had the usual vanities—but he was kind and polite, not someone who made enemies."

"Not at all," I agreed.

"In early summer of 1811, he got permission to copy a painting in one of these rooms and came to Versailles to do it. He worked slowly. Then he left his hotel and moved to the Dragon Volant—specifically choosing the very room you're in now. After that, he hardly painted or visited his Paris home.

"One night, he told the innkeeper that he was going to Paris for a few days on important business. His servant was going with him, but he'd be back soon and wanted to keep the room. He left some clothes behind, packed a bag and his toiletries, got into his carriage with his servant, and left for Paris.

"You're following all this, Monsieur?"

"Very closely," I said.

"Well, sir," Carmaignac said, "when they were almost at his home, the Count suddenly told his servant to stop the carriage. He said he had changed his mind and wouldn't sleep there that night. He explained he had important business up north, near Rouen, and needed to leave before sunrise. He'd be gone for about two weeks.

He flagged down a cab, picked up a leather bag that, according to the servant, was only big enough for a few shirts and a coat—but felt incredibly heavy. The servant held it while the Count took out his wallet and counted thirty-six gold coins for him to take care of while he was away. Then the Count sent the servant on in the carriage, and he got into the cab with the heavy bag. That's where things start to get strange."

"I'm following," I said.

"Now here's the mystery," Carmaignac continued. "After that night, Count Chateau Blassemare was never seen again. Nobody— friend or stranger—ever heard from him. The day before he vanished, he had asked his stockbroker to sell all his investments and give him the money in cash. He told the broker he needed the money to deal with some financial matters up north. That bag, which the servant thought was oddly heavy, probably held a lot of gold."

He paused to offer me some snuff, which I tried out of politeness.

"A reward was offered during the investigation. The ad called for any cab driver who had worked around 10:30 that night and picked up a man with a black leather bag who had gotten out of a private carriage and paid his servant. Around 150 cab drivers came forward, but none matched. Still, we got a strange and unexpected clue from a completely different source. What a racket that annoying harlequin is making with his sword!"

"Totally unbearable!" I said.

Once the noisy clown left, Carmaignac went on.

"The clue came from a boy, about twelve years old, who knew the Count well because he had delivered messages for him before. He said that around 12:30 that same night—under a bright full moon—he was sent to get a midwife because his mother suddenly got sick. His house was about a mile or more from the Dragon Volant, and to get to the midwife, he had to pass the back of the Château de la Carque. The road runs by the old cemetery of St. Aubin, which is only separated from the road by a short fence and a few giant old trees.

As he walked past, nervous in the moonlight, he saw a man he swore was the Count. Locals called him 'the man of smiles,' but he didn't look cheerful now. He was sitting on a tombstone, with one pistol resting on it while he loaded another. The boy tiptoed past, terrified but watching him the whole time. He said the clothes were different from what the Count usually wore, but he was absolutely sure it was him. The face was serious, but still the same. He never changed his story. If it really was him, that was the last time anyone saw the Count. No one ever found any trace of him in Rouen, or anywhere else. No death was recorded. No sign of life either."

"That really is a strange story," I said, and was about to ask more questions when Tom Whistlewick returned. I hadn't noticed him wander off, but now he looked more awake—and much less tipsy.

"I say, Carmaignac, it's getting late. I really must leave, for the reason I told you earlier. Beckett, we'll meet again soon," he said.

"I'm sorry I can't tell you the second story right now," said Carmaignac, "but it's about another guest who stayed in the same room you're in—a case even more bizarre and unsettling than the one I just described. It happened later that same year."

"Would you both do me a favor and come have dinner with me at the Dragon Volant tomorrow?" I asked as we walked together through the Galerie des Glaces. They agreed.

"By Jove!" said Whistlewick. "Look at that weird pagoda—no, wait, sedan chair—over there! The one they just left sitting by itself. Not a single one of those fortune tellers is near it now. I still can't figure out how they predict things so well. Jack Nuffles—met him here earlier—says they're gypsies. I wonder where they went? I'm going to peek inside."

He tried pulling at the blinds on the strange chair, which were made like Venetian blinds, with red curtains behind them. One blind didn't fully close, so he peeked through it.

When he came back, he said, "It's too dark to see much, but I did spot the old guy in there. He's wearing gold and red, and some fancy hat like a mandarin's. He's asleep. And by Jove, does he stink! Smells like a skunk! Just seeing him was worth it for the story. Whew! Yuck!"

I wasn't too interested in smelling that for myself, so we slowly made our way to the exit. I reminded them of their dinner promise, then headed to my carriage. Soon I was riding alone along the quiet road back to the Dragon Volant, under old trees and soft moonlight.

So much had happened in just a couple of hours. So many strange and vivid moments packed into such a short time. And now, something wild was waiting for me ahead.

The peaceful, moonlit road was a sharp contrast to the lights, music, and chaos of the party I had just left. Nature at that hour had a calming effect. For a moment, I felt guilty and uneasy about the risky path I was on. I wished I had never gotten into this strange mess—but it was too late to turn back. A bitter feeling crept in, and for a few minutes, my heart felt heavy. I almost felt like spilling everything to my cheerful friend Alfred Ogle—or even to the easygoing Tom Whistlewick.

Chapter XVI.
The Parc of the Château De La Carque

There was no risk that the Dragon Volant would shut its doors early that night. Many of the guests' servants were staying there, and since their wealthy employers wouldn't be leaving the ball until very late, the inn would stay open until at least three or four in the morning. That meant I had plenty of time for my secret meeting without worrying about being locked out or raising suspicion.

We stopped beneath the overhanging trees, right in front of the Dragon Volant, where the light from the entrance glowed warmly. I sent my carriage away, ran up the wide staircase, still holding my mask, with my costume fluttering around me, and stepped into my large, shadowy room. The dark wood walls and old-fashioned furniture, along with the tall bed draped in heavy curtains, made the room feel even gloomier.

A slanted patch of moonlight shone on the floor through the window, which I hurried to. Outside, everything was quiet and glowing under the soft moonlight. I could see the silhouette of the Château de la Carque in the distance—its chimneys and towers stood out black against the pale sky. A bit closer, just to the left, I spotted the small clump of trees that the masked lady had pointed out as the secret meeting place. It was halfway between my window and the château.

I studied that little grove carefully, memorizing its shape and position under the moon. My heart was beating faster just thinking about what might happen there.

But time was passing quickly. I threw off my costume and shoes, replaced them with boots, put on my hat, and finally took a pair of pistols with me—people had warned me that the roads weren't always safe, with bands of former soldiers wandering around. After checking my appearance once more in the mirror by the moonlight, I went downstairs.

In the front hall, I called for my servant.

"St. Clair," I said, "I'm going out for a short walk in the moonlight—just ten minutes or so. Stay up until I get back. If it's a beautiful night, I might walk a little longer."

Then I casually stepped outside, pretending to be unsure of which way to go. I strolled up the road, glancing up at the moon and whistling a tune I'd heard at the theater.

After I'd walked a few hundred yards, I stopped whistling and turned around to check the road. It glowed pale under the moonlight. I could still see the roof of the Dragon Volant, and one window lit faintly behind the leaves.

There were no footsteps, no sign of anyone nearby. I checked my watch in the moonlight—it was just eight minutes until the meeting time. A thick patch of ivy covered part of the wall nearby, reaching the top and making it easier to climb. It also helped hide me in case anyone looked my way.

I climbed over and landed inside the grounds of the château—now officially trespassing.

Ahead of me, the dark grove rose like a wall of shadows. It looked bigger and darker with every step I took. Soon I reached it and stepped inside, glad for the cover.

Inside the grove, there was a small clearing near the middle. In that space stood a little Greek-style temple with steps all around it and a statue in the center. The white marble building had tall, fluted columns. Grass and moss grew between the cracks, and everything looked old and forgotten. In front of it, a fountain trickled softly into a wide marble basin. The water shimmered like silver in the moonlight.

The temple and fountain were hauntingly beautiful, and their worn-down look made the scene feel even more magical—like something from a fairy tale.

But I didn't focus on all that. I was too busy watching the path from the château, waiting for the Countess.

Suddenly, a voice spoke near my left shoulder. I turned quickly—and there was the masked woman in the same costume as before, dressed like Mademoiselle de la Vallière.

"The Countess will be here soon," she said.

She stood in the open moonlight, and her figure looked more graceful than ever.

"In the meantime," she continued, "let me tell you a bit more about her situation. She's miserable, trapped in a marriage with a jealous man who now wants to force her to sell her diamonds, which are—"

"Worth thirty thousand pounds," I said. "I heard all about that from a friend. But can I help her somehow? If there's danger, I don't care. If there's any way I can assist her, just tell me. I'll do it."

"If you don't fear danger—or don't see it as danger," she said, "and if you care nothing for society's rules, and if you're brave enough to support a woman with nothing to gain for yourself but her thanks, then yes—you can help her. You could earn not only her thanks but a special place in her heart."

She turned away and looked like she was crying.

I swore I'd do anything for the Countess. "But," I said, "you told me she would be here."

"Yes," she answered, "unless something unexpected happens. With the Count de St. Alyre in the house and always watching, it's not always safe for her to leave."

"Does she really want to see me?" I asked, my voice a little unsure.

"First tell me—have you really thought about her since that night at the Belle Étoile?"

"She's never left my mind. Day and night, I see her eyes and hear her voice."

"People say my voice sounds like hers," said the masked woman.

"It does," I admitted. "But only a little."

"Oh? Maybe mine's better, then?"

"I didn't mean that," I said quickly. "Your voice is very sweet. I just think hers is a little softer."

"A little higher-pitched, you mean?" she said, sounding annoyed.

"No, not high-pitched. Yours is lovely, just not as emotional."

"That's just your bias," she replied. "It's not true."

I gave a polite bow. I didn't want to argue with her.

"So, you think I'm full of myself?" she said. "You're mocking me because I dare to compare myself to the Countess de St. Alyre. Well then—look at my hand. Can you honestly say hers is more beautiful than mine?"

She pulled off her glove and held out her hand in the moonlight.

She looked really upset now. It felt awkward—and frustrating. The minutes were slipping away, and instead of talking about anything important, we were stuck in this silly back-and-forth.

"Well?" she pressed. "Isn't my hand as beautiful as hers?"

"I can't say that," I replied, a bit annoyed. "I'm not going to compare. But to me, the Countess de St. Alyre is the most beautiful woman I've ever seen."

The masked woman gave a cold laugh, then sighed. "I'll prove I'm right." And with that, she took off her mask—and there she was. The Countess herself, smiling, blushing, and more stunning than ever.

"Good heavens!" I gasped. "How incredibly stupid I've been. I was talking to Madame la Comtesse the whole time at the ball!"

I stared at her, speechless. She laughed softly, kindly, and offered me her hand. I took it and gently kissed it.

"No, not yet," she said, smiling. "We're not that close—yet. But I can see it now. You do remember me from the Belle Étoile. And you're loyal and brave. If you had fallen for the fake rivalry of Mademoiselle de la Vallière just now, I wouldn't have trusted you again. But I do trust you. Now you know—I haven't forgotten you either. And if you would risk your life for me, I'd take risks too, just to keep from losing you."

She paused and looked into my eyes.

"I can't stay long. Will you come back tomorrow night, at a quarter past eleven? I'll be here, exactly on time. But you must be very careful. No one can know. You must promise me that."

I swore again and again that I'd rather die than let anyone find out.

She looked more beautiful with every passing second. I was completely under her spell.

"Tomorrow," she continued, "take a different path. And next time, we'll change it again. On the far side of the château, there's an old graveyard with a ruined chapel. People are too scared to go there at night. There's a path that leads into the park. Follow it. You'll find a thick patch of bushes—only fifty steps from here."

I promised to follow her directions exactly.

"I've spent more than a year unsure of what to do," she said quietly. "But now I've made up my mind. My life has been sad. It's been lonelier than life in a convent. I've had no one to talk to, no one to help me, no one to pull me out of this miserable life. But now I've found a brave and ready friend."

Her voice became softer. "Do you think I could ever forget what you did for me at the Belle Étoile? Do you still have the rose I gave you that night? Yes? You swear? You don't have to—I believe you. Richard. I've whispered your name so many times when I've been alone. Richard, my hero. Oh, Richard… I love you!"

I was about to fall to my knees, to hold her close—but she stopped me.

"No. We can't waste time on emotions. You must understand. In marriage, there's no such thing as feeling nothing. If you don't love your husband, you end up hating him. And the Count—though he may seem silly—is dangerously jealous. So for my sake, be careful. If anyone mentions the Count or the Countess de St. Alyre, act like you've never met us. I'll tell you more tomorrow. I have reasons for everything I do—and for everything I wait to do. Now go. Please."

She stepped back and signaled me to leave. I said goodbye and followed her instructions.

The meeting hadn't lasted more than ten minutes. I climbed back over the wall and returned to the Dragon Volant before they shut the doors.

That night, I couldn't sleep. My heart was racing. I lay awake, replaying everything she had said. I saw her again and again in my mind, always standing in the moonlight.

Chapter XVII.
The Tenant of the Palanquin

The Marquis came to see me the next day. I was still finishing a late breakfast when he arrived. He said he needed a favor. His carriage had been damaged in the crowd after the ball, and he asked if he could ride with me to Paris. I was already planning to go, and I was happy to have his company.

He came with me to my hotel, and we went up to my room. I was surprised to see someone already there, sitting in a chair with his back to us, reading a newspaper. He stood up—it was Count de St. Alyre. He wore gold-rimmed glasses, and his oily black wig clung to his head like shiny wood. His scarf was pulled down, and one arm was in a sling. I couldn't tell if his face looked more unpleasant than usual, or if it was just because of everything I'd learned about him during my strange meeting in the park—but something about him felt more menacing than before.

I wasn't used to hiding guilt, and seeing him so suddenly made me uneasy.

He smiled.

"I stopped by hoping to find you, Monsieur Beckett," he said in a croaky voice. "I was thinking of asking you a favor, though it might be a bit much. But perhaps my friend, the Marquis d'Harmonville, will help me instead."

"With pleasure," said the Marquis, "but not until after six. I have a meeting with three or four people I can't miss. We won't be done any earlier."

"What a shame," said the Count. "I only needed an hour. Such bad luck!"

"I can give you an hour," I offered.

"How kind of you, Monsieur. I didn't expect that. The task is a bit gloomy for someone as young and lively as you. Here, read this note I got this morning."

The note was definitely not cheerful. It explained that the body of the Count's cousin, Monsieur de St. Amand, who had died at his home (the Château Clery), would be sent for burial at Père Lachaise Cemetery, according to his wishes. With the Count's permission, it would arrive at the Château de la Carque around ten o'clock the next night to be taken by hearse to the cemetery, along with any relatives who wished to attend.

"I only met the poor man twice," said the Count. "But I'm his only relative, and I couldn't say no. I need to visit the cemetery office to sign some papers and confirm the arrangements. But I've injured my thumb and can't sign anything for a week. Luckily, any name will do. Yours will work just fine. Since you're coming with me, everything will go smoothly."

We drove off together. The Count gave me a note with the cousin's full name, age, cause of death, and instructions for a simple grave to be dug between two family vaults. The burial was set for 1:30 a.m. the night after next. He also handed me a large sum of money to cover night burial fees. I asked who the receipt should be made out to.

"Not me, my friend," he said. "They wanted me to be the executor of the will, which I refused in writing yesterday. But if the receipt's in my name, I might be legally considered the executor. Take it in your name, if you don't mind."

So I did.

You'll soon understand why these details matter.

While I took care of the paperwork, the Count stayed in the carriage. When I returned, he was still there, dozing, with his scarf pulled up and his hat low over his eyes.

Paris no longer excited me. I rushed through the little I had to do and found myself longing for my quiet room at the Dragon Volant, the dark woods around the Château de la Carque, and the thrilling feeling of being close to the woman I was hopelessly—but foolishly—falling for.

I was held up a bit by my stockbroker. I had a large sum of money sitting in the bank. Normally I wouldn't care about a few days of lost interest—but at that point, I hardly cared about the money at all. The only thing I cared about was the woman who haunted my every thought, calling me back through the shadows toward the whispering trees of the château.

I had planned to meet the broker that day, and I was relieved when he advised me to leave the money where it was for now. He said the market was about to drop. Oddly enough, that delay would also end up playing a part in everything that happened afterward.

When I got back to the Dragon Volant, I was annoyed to find my two dinner guests already waiting in the sitting room. I had completely forgotten about them. I silently blamed myself for agreeing to meet them—it was too late to back out now. I gave the waiter a quick word to get dinner started.

Tom Whistlewick was full of energy and immediately began telling a strange story.

He said that not just Versailles, but all of Paris was buzzing about a disturbing and nearly sacrilegious prank that had happened the night before. The pagoda—he kept calling the Chinese-style palanquin by that name—had been left exactly where we had last seen it. The conjuror, his assistant, and the four carriers had never returned.

When the ball ended and everyone finally left, the staff came in to put out the lights and lock up. They found the palanquin still sitting there. Thinking someone would come for it in the morning, they decided to leave it overnight.

But the next day, no one came.

Eventually, the staff was told to move it. Only then did they notice how unusually heavy it was. That reminded them of the man inside. They forced the door open—and were horrified to find not a living person, but a dead body inside. The man in the Chinese robe and painted hat had been dead for at least three or four days.

Some believed the prank was meant as an insult to the Allied guests, since the ball had been thrown in their honor. Others thought it was just a tasteless joke—something wild and shocking pulled off by reckless young people. But a smaller group, more superstitious, believed the dead body was actually part of the act, and that the strange things people had heard from the conjuror had come from real magic.

"The police are handling the case now," said Monsieur Carmaignac. "And we aren't the same slow-moving force we used to be. Whoever did this will be found—unless they were much smarter than fools like that usually are."

I sat quietly, still thinking about the strange conversation I'd had with the supposed conjuror. Carmaignac had called him a fool, but to me, it all seemed far too detailed and strange to be explained away like that. The more I thought about it, the more unbelievable it seemed.

"It was definitely a strange kind of joke," said Whistlewick, "but I'm not sure what the point was."

"Not even a new idea," said Carmaignac. "Almost the same thing happened over a hundred years ago at another fancy ball in Paris. The people behind that trick were never caught either."

As I later found in one of my old books of French stories, Carmaignac had been right. I'd even marked that very story myself.

While we were still talking, the waiter came in to say dinner was ready. We headed to the dining room, and thankfully, my guests had enough energy to carry the conversation without much help from me.

Chapter XVIII.
The Churchyard

Our dinner turned out to be excellent—so was the wine. Honestly, it was better than what I'd had at some fancy hotels in Paris. A really good meal has a powerful effect on people. We all felt calmer and in a better mood afterward. It was a steady, pleasant kind of happiness—more lasting than the loud joy that comes from drinking too much.

My friends were cheerful and talkative, which was great for me. It meant I didn't have to say much and could just sit back while they kept the conversation going with story after story. To be honest, I wasn't paying much attention—my thoughts were elsewhere—until suddenly, something caught my interest.

"Yes," Carmaignac was saying, continuing a conversation I had mostly missed, "there was another case, even stranger than the Russian noble's. I remembered it earlier but couldn't recall the man's name. He stayed in the exact same room, by the way—the one you're in now." He turned to me with a half-joking smile. "Maybe you should ask for a different room now that the place isn't so full—unless you plan to disappear too."

"Thanks," I said with a laugh, "but no. I might switch hotels soon anyway. And I'm not too worried about vanishing—at least not yet. But you said there's another story tied to that room? I'd love to hear it. But first, have some more wine."

He told the story.

"It happened before the other two cases," Carmaignac said. "A Frenchman—his name slips my mind—came to stay at the Dragon Volant. He was the son of a merchant, and the innkeeper gave him the same room we've been talking about—your room. He wasn't young, maybe over forty, and definitely not attractive. The locals said he was the ugliest but kindest man they ever met. He played the violin, wrote poetry, and sang. His habits were odd. Sometimes he stayed in his room all day, playing and writing, and only went out for a walk at night. A real eccentric."

"He wasn't super rich, but he had a fair amount—over half a million francs. He talked to his stockbroker about investing in foreign bonds and pulled all his money out of the bank. That's where things get strange."

"Refill your glass first," I said.

"Dutch courage to handle the mystery!" said Whistlewick, topping off his wine.

Carmaignac continued. "That night, the man told the landlord not to let anyone disturb him. He said he was finally starting his long-planned epic poem. He had two pairs of candles, a small dinner on a side table, and everything set up—ink, pens, piles of paper. When a waiter brought him coffee at nine, he was furiously writing. He didn't even look up. But when the waiter came back half an hour later, the door was locked. The man said not to bother him again."

"The next morning, the waiter knocked again—no answer. He looked through the keyhole. The candles were still burning, the shutters were closed, just like the night before. No reply, even after louder knocking. So he told the innkeeper, who found a key that opened the door. Inside, the room was empty. The bed hadn't been touched. The shutters were still barred. The man had vanished."

"But that wasn't the only odd thing. The Dragon Volant locks up tight at midnight—no one can leave after that without a key. And if someone had taken a key, the innkeeper should have noticed, since he kept them above his bed. He swore they hadn't been touched."

"There was one more clue," Carmaignac said. "A servant, not knowing the man didn't want to be disturbed, had knocked around 12:30, after everything was locked up. He saw a light under the door and heard the poet shout to leave him alone. So we know he was in the room after the place was sealed for the night."

"And that's the last anyone ever saw of him?" I asked.

"Exactly. He never showed up again. No clues, no body, no money—nothing. Either he died or something happened that forced him to disappear completely. But all we know for sure is that he stayed in your room and vanished, just like the others."

"So that makes three people," I said, "all vanishing from the same room."

"Yes," said Carmaignac. "And not one of their bodies was ever found. When someone's murdered, hiding the body is always the hardest part. So how could three people in a row vanish like that without leaving any trace?"

After that, we moved on to lighter topics. Carmaignac shared a bunch of wild and scandalous stories he'd picked up during his time working with the police.

Thankfully, both of my guests had plans in Paris and left around ten o'clock.

I went up to my room and looked out the window toward the Château de la Carque. The moon kept slipping behind clouds, and the view of the park below looked strange and gloomy in the flickering light.

The strange stories Monsieur Carmaignac told me about the room I was in came back to me suddenly. They pushed aside the funnier tales he told afterward and filled my mind with a shadowy unease. I looked around the dark room and felt a little uncomfortable. I picked up my pistols with a strange sense that maybe I'd actually need them tonight. That thought didn't scare me, though—it only made me more excited. My mission completely absorbed me, and now it carried a thrill that felt serious and intense.

I stayed in my room for a while. I had already figured out exactly where the little graveyard was—it was about a mile away. I didn't want to get there too early.

I slipped out quietly and walked down the road to my left, then turned onto a smaller path that curved around the edge of the park. Tall old trees lined the path, and soon I reached the graveyard. It was a small place, hidden among trees, barely larger than half an acre, and it sat between the road and the Château de la Carque's park.

I stopped and listened. It was completely quiet. A thick cloud had covered the moon, so I couldn't see much—just the vague shapes of nearby things. Every now and then, the white face of a tombstone would stand out from the dark.

Some of the shapes I saw against the grey sky looked like tall shrubs, something like little poplar trees or yews. I didn't know what they were, but I'd seen them before in graveyards.

I knew I was early, so I sat on the edge of a tombstone to wait. Maybe the Countess had a good reason for not wanting me to enter the château grounds before the exact time she'd given. I sat there in that lazy, half-aware way people do when they're waiting, staring at a dark shape in front of me. It was only a few steps away.

As the moon slowly came out from behind the clouds, I realized the shape I'd been staring at wasn't a tree at all. It was a man. He was standing perfectly still. The light grew brighter, and soon I could see him clearly. It was Colonel Gaillarde. Thankfully, he wasn't looking at me. I could only see the side of his face, but I recognized the white mustache, the sharp features, and his tall, lean figure. He stood with his shoulder toward me, clearly waiting for someone or watching for a signal.

If he turned and saw me, I knew I'd have to fight him again—just like at the Belle Étoile. Of all the people who could have shown up, he was the worst. If he found out what I was doing, he'd be thrilled to ruin me—and the Countess, too, since he clearly hated her.

Then he raised his arm and gave a soft whistle. A moment later, I heard another whistle in reply. I was relieved when he started walking toward the sound, moving farther away with each step. Soon I heard voices, quiet and cautious. One of them sounded like Gaillarde.

I crept after them carefully, making sure I stayed hidden. I thought I saw the shape of a hat above a broken wall, and then another beside it—two men talking. They walked away, not toward the park, but toward the road. I lay down in the grass behind a grave, watching them like a scout. One by one, they climbed over the stile at the edge of the road. The Colonel was last. He paused on the wall, looking around, then jumped down and followed his companion. I listened to their footsteps and voices growing fainter as they walked farther from the Dragon Volant.

Once I was sure they were gone, I entered the park. I followed the Countess's instructions carefully, moving through thick brush and low trees until I reached the edge of the open space near the ruined temple. I crossed quickly.

Now I was under the huge branches of the old lime and chestnut trees again. My heart beat fast as I approached the little temple.

The moonlight poured down through the trees, lighting up patches of grass and casting shadows.

I reached the steps. I stepped among the old marble columns. She wasn't there—not inside, and not in the center space behind the ivy-covered windows.

The Countess hadn't arrived yet.

Chapter XIX.
The Key

I stood on the temple steps, watching and listening. After a minute or two, I heard the crunch of dry twigs being stepped on. I looked toward the sound and saw someone walking through the trees, wrapped in a cloak.

I stepped forward quickly—it was the Countess. She didn't say a word but gave me her hand, and I led her back to where we had last spoken. She stopped my excited greeting with gentle but firm calmness. Then she pulled back her hood, letting her beautiful hair fall loose, and looked at me with glowing, sad eyes. She sighed deeply. Something serious was clearly on her mind.

"Richard," she said, "I need to speak honestly. This is the most important moment of my life. I know you would protect me. I think you feel sorry for me—maybe you even love me."

Like any lovestruck young man, I began to speak passionately. But she quieted me again with that same sad determination.

"Listen to me, dear friend, and then decide if you can help. I'm trusting you in a way that seems crazy—and yet my heart tells me I'm right to do so. Meeting you here like this—how reckless it seems! You must think badly of me. But once you know everything, I hope you'll understand. I can't do this alone. If I fail, I'll have nothing left. I'm married to a man I can't respect—someone I despise. I've decided to run away. I have jewelry—mostly diamonds—worth thirty thousand pounds in English money. I was offered that amount for them. They belong to me; I kept them in my name when I married. I'm going to take them with me. You probably know something about jewels. I was looking over mine when it was time to meet you, and I brought this to show."

She held up a diamond necklace, and it sparkled in the moonlight as it dangled from her fingers. Even in such a dramatic moment, I noticed the joy she seemed to get from showing it off.

"It's beautiful," I said.

"Yes," she replied. "But I'll give them all up. I'll sell them and break the cruel tie that traps me. A man like you—young, handsome, brave, and generous—probably isn't rich. Richard, if you love me like you say you do, then come with me. We'll escape to Switzerland. We'll stay ahead of anyone chasing us. Powerful friends will help us and get us separated legally. Then we'll be free to be happy. You'll have earned that happiness—you'll have saved me."

You can imagine how passionately I responded. I promised her everything—my loyalty, my help, my life.

"Tomorrow night," she continued, "my husband is going to escort the body of his cousin, Monsieur de St. Amand, to Père la Chaise. The hearse will leave here at half-past nine. Be here where we're standing by nine."

I swore I'd be there on time.

"I won't meet you here," she said, pointing. "But do you see that red light in the window of the tower, there at the corner of the château?"

I nodded.

"I placed it there on purpose. Tomorrow night, when you see that red light appear, it means the funeral has left. It will be safe to come. Go to that window—I'll open it and let you in. Five minutes later, a carriage with four horses will be ready at the gate. I'll give you the diamonds, and once we get in the carriage, we'll be on our way. We'll have at least five hours' lead. If we act quickly and wisely, we'll be fine. Will you do all this for me?"

Again, I promised to do anything for her.

"My only worry," she added, "is how we'll quickly turn my diamonds into money. I can't move them while my husband is still in the house."

This was the moment I had been waiting for. I told her I already had thirty thousand pounds at my banker's, and I could bring the whole amount in gold and notes. That way she wouldn't need to rush to sell her diamonds at a loss.

"Heavens!" she said, almost disappointed. "So you're rich? Then I won't get to help my brave friend by sharing what I have. But if that's the case, let us share what we both have—your money and my jewels. It makes me happy to mix our fortunes together."

That led to a very romantic exchange—full of emotion and dreamy talk, which I won't try to repeat here.

Then she gave me a very important instruction.

"I also brought a key," she said, "and I need to explain how to use it."

It was a long key, with two different ends—one like a regular door key, and the other small, like for a jewelry box.

"You can't be too careful tomorrow night. Any interruption could ruin everything. I found out you're staying in the haunted room at the Dragon Volant. That's perfect. I'll tell you why—years ago, a man stayed in that room and vanished overnight. The truth is, he ran away from his debts, and the innkeeper helped him escape. My husband looked into it and found out how he did it. It was with this key. Here's a note and a drawing that explains how to use it. I took them from the Count's desk."

She handed me the papers.

"Now it's up to you to fool the staff at the Dragon Volant. Test the keys first to make sure the locks work smoothly. I'll have my jewels ready. And you should bring your money with you—once we leave, it could be a long time before you return to Paris or let anyone know where we are. As for our passports—arrange everything: the names, the destination—whatever you decide. And now, dear Richard…"

She leaned her arm on my shoulder and looked deeply into my eyes, holding my hand tightly.

"My life is in your hands. I'm trusting you with everything."

Just as she said this, her face turned pale. She gasped, "Oh no— who's there?"

Just as she spoke, the Countess quickly stepped back through a door in the marble wall behind her. It led into a small room without a roof, as tiny as the shrine itself. The only window there was almost completely covered by thick ivy, so barely any moonlight could get in.

I stood right at the doorway she had just passed through, looking toward the direction of the glance that had made her so scared. I understood why she was afraid. Less than twenty yards away, coming straight toward us in the moonlight, were Colonel Gaillarde and another man. They were walking quickly, clearly visible.

I was standing partly in the shadow of the wall and cornice and didn't even realize how well hidden I was. I expected the Colonel to suddenly shout and come charging toward me.

I stepped back quietly, pulled one of my pistols from my pocket, and cocked it. I was ready. If he tried to enter that room where the Countess was hiding, I was prepared to shoot him. It would have been murder, yes—but at that moment, I felt no guilt. Once you start down a path of secrets and wrong choices, you're closer to worse crimes than you might think.

"There's the statue," said the Colonel in his usual harsh tone.

"The one mentioned in the poem?" asked the other man.

"That's the one. We'll see more next time. Come on, Monsieur—let's go."

To my great relief, the Colonel turned around and walked off, heading through the trees toward the wall at the edge of the park. They climbed over it not far from the Dragon Volant.

When I returned to the little room, I found the Countess still shaking with fear—this time very real, not put on. She refused to let me walk her back toward the château. But I promised her I would keep the Colonel away and that she had nothing to fear from him now.

She began to calm down. She gave me a warm and lingering goodnight, then left. I stood there for a long time, watching her disappear into the night. I held the key in my hand and felt like I was drifting through a dream—like I was slipping into madness.

There I was, ready to risk everything—rules, laws, my own soul. I was willing to commit murder if I had to, all because of a woman I barely knew. All I really knew was that she was beautiful and bold.

To this day, I often thank God for guiding me safely out of that maze of lies and danger—one I almost couldn't escape.

Chapter XX.

A High-Cauld-Cap

I was now back on the road, just a few hundred yards from the Dragon Volant. I had really gotten myself into something serious! And to top it off, I might be walking right into another run-in with that strange, sword-swinging Colonel at the inn—though I might not be as lucky this time.

I was glad I had my pistols with me. I didn't see any reason why I should let a madman attack me without defending myself.

The road to the inn looked beautiful under the moonlight, with low-hanging branches from the old park trees on one side and tall poplars on the other. But I wasn't really focused on the scenery. My thoughts were all over the place. So much had happened so fast, and I had gotten myself tangled up in something wild and dangerous. It hardly felt real. As I slowly walked toward the open door of the Dragon Volant, I didn't even feel like the same person anymore.

Luckily, there was no sign of the Colonel—no sight or sound of him. I asked at the front hall if anyone new had arrived in the past thirty minutes, and they said no. I checked the public room, but it was empty. The clock struck midnight, and I heard the servant locking the front door. I picked up my candle and went upstairs. All the lights in the inn were out by then. The place felt quiet and sleepy.

As I reached the landing, the moonlight streamed through a window and lit up the stairs. I stopped for a moment to look outside. I could see the trees and towers of the château, which now meant so much to me. But I quickly remembered that someone might see me and think I was signaling—maybe even the Count himself, watching with jealous suspicion. So I moved on.

When I opened the door to my room, I was startled to see an old woman standing there. She had the longest face I'd ever seen and wore a high, old-fashioned cap. Its white lace only made her wrinkled skin look darker. Her eyes were oddly bright, almost too dark, and her shoulders were hunched.

"I lit a little fire, Monsieur," she said, her voice shaky. "It's cold tonight."

I thanked her, expecting her to leave, but she didn't. She just stood there, holding her candle.

"Forgive an old woman," she said, "but what could a young English lord like you—who could have all of Paris—possibly find interesting here at the Dragon Volant?"

If I'd been a kid still reading fairy tales, I might've thought she was a wicked witch or a spirit of the place, here to warn me. But even though I was older now, something about her gave me the creeps. Her eyes stared straight into mine like she knew everything. I started to feel nervous. Somehow, I knew she had figured out my secret.

"I saw you tonight," she said calmly. "In the park at the château."

"Me?" I said, pretending to be shocked.

"It's no use pretending, Monsieur. I know why you're here. I'm telling you: leave. Go tomorrow morning, and don't come back."

She raised her free hand, looking at me like she was warning me of something terrible.

"I don't know what you're talking about," I said. "And even if I did, why would it matter to you?"

"It doesn't matter to me," she said coldly. "But it matters to the honor of a noble family I once served, back when being noble still meant something. But fine—ignore my warning. Keep your secret, and I'll keep mine. You'll find out soon enough how hard it is to hold onto it."

And with that, the old woman left, slowly closing the door behind her. I stood there, frozen in place, not sure what to say or do. I didn't move for nearly five minutes.

I figured she must be terrified of the Count's jealousy and had come to warn me off. Still, I hated the idea that someone—even this strange old woman—might know about the Countess and me. And worse, that she might be on the Count's side.

Should I warn the Countess? She had trusted me so completely, maybe I owed her that. But what if trying to reach her only made things worse? What had the old woman meant when she said, "Keep your secret, and I'll keep mine"?

I couldn't stop thinking. A thousand questions spun in my head. Every step I took seemed to bring new danger, like walking through a dark forest full of traps and monsters I couldn't see until they were right in front of me.

I forced myself to stop thinking about all those scary and confusing thoughts. I locked my door, sat at the table, and placed a candle on each side of me. Then I took out the piece of parchment that showed the drawings and notes. These were my instructions for using the key.

After studying the directions for a while, I began my search. At the right-hand corner of the room, near the window, the wooden paneling made a slanted turn. I looked at it closely. When I pressed a certain spot, a small part of the wood frame slid aside and revealed a hidden keyhole. When I removed my finger, it clicked back into place on its own. So far, I had followed the instructions correctly.

Next, I searched near the door, just beneath the other keyhole. I found another hidden keyhole in the paneling. The small end of the double key fit into it perfectly, just like it had upstairs. I gave it a few hard turns, and soon a panel swung open, revealing a section of plain wall and a narrow, arched opening cut into the thick stone. Inside was a stone spiral staircase.

Holding a candle, I stepped into the passage. The air had a strange, damp smell—like something that hadn't been touched in years. The candle lit up the cold stone walls around me as I carefully made my way down the stairs. After several turns, I reached the bottom, where there was an old wooden door, deeply set into the thick wall. I used the larger end of the key this time. The lock was stiff, so I had to set my candle down and use both hands to turn it. As it turned, the lock made a loud creaking sound that startled me—I was afraid someone might hear.

I stood still for a few minutes, just in case, then slowly pushed the door open. A cool breeze rushed in and blew out my candle. Outside, thick holly bushes and tangled branches pressed right up to the door. Without the candle, it was almost pitch-black, except for tiny bits of moonlight slipping through the leaves above.

Moving quietly so I wouldn't be heard, I pushed through the thick plants until I saw open ground. I realized the brush stretched far up into the park and connected with the wooded area near the little marble temple where I had met the Countess before.

No general could've picked a better hidden path from the Dragon Volant to that secret meeting spot.

When I looked back, I noticed the staircase I had used was built inside one of the tall, narrow towers decorating the inn. It was placed exactly where the map had shown—in line with the wall panel in my room.

Feeling proud that everything had worked as planned, I returned through the hidden door, climbed the stairs, and went back into my room. I locked the secret panel again, kissed the key the Countess had given me, and placed it under my pillow.

Soon after, I lay down with my spinning thoughts. It took me a while to finally fall asleep.

Chapter XXI.
I See Three Men In A Mirror

I woke up very early the next morning, too excited to fall back asleep. As soon as it seemed normal to be up and about, I found the innkeeper and told him a story I had made up. I said I was heading into Paris that night and then traveling on for business, so if anyone asked, he should say I'd be gone for about a week. I added that my servant, St. Clair, would keep the room key and watch over my belongings while I was away.

With that cover story set, I headed into Paris to deal with my money. My goal was to turn nearly thirty thousand pounds into something I could easily carry and use wherever I ended up—without needing to write letters or give away my location. I was able to handle that without much trouble. There's no need to explain the passport part, except to say I'd chosen a peaceful, hidden town in Switzerland as our escape spot.

I wasn't going to take any luggage. We'd buy what we needed the next morning in the first big town we came to. After I finished everything, I looked at the clock—it was only two in the afternoon. Just two! And I had no idea how to kill the rest of the day.

I realized I'd never visited Notre Dame Cathedral, so I went and spent over an hour there. Then I stopped by the Conciergerie, the Palais de Justice, and the Sainte-Chapelle. Still, I had time to spare, so I wandered the narrow old streets nearby. In one, I saw a sign on an old house that said it had once belonged to Canon Fulbert, the uncle of the famous Héloïse. I don't know if those streets still exist, but they were filled with historic buildings—some now used as warehouses.

Eventually, I wandered into a dusty little shop full of old furniture, armor, china, and decorations. The shopkeeper was busy polishing a piece of armor and let me browse freely. As I moved toward the back, I came across a dirty old window and turned around. In an alcove off to the side, I saw a large mirror with a worn wooden frame. In its reflection, I noticed a hidden nook cluttered with junk. At a table sat three men, deep in conversation.

To my shock, I instantly recognized two of them: Colonel Gaillarde and the Marquis d'Harmonville. The third was a thin, pale man with smallpox scars and oily black hair—he looked shady and untrustworthy. The Marquis looked up, and the other two quickly followed. I froze. But luckily, they didn't recognize me. I was standing in shadow, with the light behind me.

Realizing I hadn't been seen, I acted like I was still looking at the items in the shop and slowly walked back toward the front. I paused to listen—no one followed me. You can bet I left that shop as fast as I could.

It wasn't my place to wonder why the Marquis and the Colonel were meeting in such a run-down place, or who that strange man was. Sometimes unusual jobs bring strange people together.

I left the shop relieved. By sunset, I had returned to the Dragon Volant. I stepped out of the carriage carrying a strong, small box, wrapped in leather to hide what was inside.

Back in my room, I called for St. Clair and told him the same story I'd told the innkeeper. Then I gave him fifty pounds for expenses and to pay for my room while I was gone. I ate a quick dinner, but I couldn't stop looking at the old clock above the fireplace. It felt like my only partner in this risky plan. The sky had turned dark with thick clouds— perfect for what I was about to do.

The innkeeper caught me in the hall to ask if I needed a ride to Paris. I had expected this question and told him I was planning to walk to Versailles and catch a carriage there.

Then I spoke to St. Clair.

"Go enjoy a bottle of wine with your friends," I told him. "I might need you later, but for now, I'll be writing some notes, so don't let anyone interrupt me for at least thirty minutes. After that, if I'm gone, just assume I've headed to Versailles. Look after everything and lock the room when I'm gone. Understand?"

He wished me well and left, likely already thinking about how he'd spend the money.

I grabbed a candle and hurried upstairs. There were only five minutes left until the time we'd agreed on. I don't think of myself as a coward, but I felt the nervous excitement of someone about to go into battle. Would I back out? Not a chance.

I locked my door, put on my coat, and placed a pistol in each pocket. Then I used the key to unlock the hidden door in the wall. I opened it a little, tucked the strong box under my arm, blew out the candle, unbolted my door, and listened to make sure no one was nearby.

Then I crossed the room quickly, stepped through the secret opening, and closed the hidden door behind me.

I stood on the winding staircase in complete darkness, holding the key. So far, everything was going exactly as planned.

Chapter XXII.
Rapture

I went down the spiral stairs in complete darkness. When I reached the stone floor, I felt around for the door and carefully found the keyhole. I opened the door with much less noise than I had the night before and stepped into the thick brush outside. It was almost just as dark there.

After closing the door behind me, I slowly pushed through the bushes, which soon became easier to move through. I stayed under the cover of the trees, walking near the edge of the woods.

Eventually, through the dark air about fifty yards ahead, I saw the pillars of the marble temple rising like ghosts through the trees. Everything seemed to be going in my favor. I had tricked both my servant and the people at the Dragon Volant, and the night was so dark that even if everyone at the inn had been suspicious, I still wouldn't have been caught—not even if they'd watched from every window.

I moved through the trees, stepping over roots, until I reached the spot where I was supposed to wait. I set my box, still wrapped in leather, on the stone ledge, and rested my arms on it while staring at the château. It was hard to see—it blended into the sky with barely any outline. Not a single window was lit. I understood that I was supposed to wait, but I had no idea for how long.

As I stood there, excited and full of hope, a strange thought suddenly crossed my mind. It felt like the air grew colder and the darkness heavier.

What if I disappeared—just like the other men in those stories? Hadn't I worked hard to hide all traces of where I really was and mislead everyone I spoke to? No one would know where I had gone.

That cold, creepy thought slipped through my mind—and then left me.

But I was still young, full of confidence, wild energy, and completely caught up in the thrill of the adventure. I had two loaded pistols—four shots—and complete belief that I could handle anything. Why worry? The Count was no threat. I had seen him scared half to death in front of that loudmouthed Colonel. What could he do?

And with someone as brave and smart as the Countess on my side, what could possibly go wrong? I laughed off the worry.

As I was thinking all this, the signal appeared. A soft pink light glowed in the window—the color of hope and the promise of a new beginning.

The stone pillars looked even darker against the light. Whispering words of love, I grabbed my strong box and quickly walked toward the Château de la Carque. There was no sign of anyone around—no lights, no voices, no footsteps, not even a dog barking. Everything was still.

When I reached the tall window, I saw that a few steps led up to it. The shutters were open like a door, and the light glowed behind a blind. A shadow moved, and then the blind was pulled aside. As I climbed the steps, I heard her soft voice say, "Richard, dearest Richard, come in! Oh, come—I've waited so long for this moment!"

She had never looked so beautiful. My heart was bursting with love for her. I almost wished there was real danger involved—she was worth risking anything for.

After our passionate greeting, she brought me to sit beside her on a couch. We talked for a few minutes. She told me the Count had left and was already over a mile away, heading with the funeral to Père la Chaise. Then she showed me her diamonds—an open case full of huge, sparkling gems.

"What's this?" she asked, looking at the box I brought.

"It holds thirty thousand pounds in cash," I said.

"All that?" she gasped.

"Every last penny."

"Was it really necessary to bring so much, when I have these?" she asked, gently touching her diamonds. "It would've made me so happy to take care of us for a while."

"My sweet, generous angel!" I said dramatically. "But remember, we might have to stay hidden for a long time. It could be too dangerous to contact anyone."

"You really brought all that money with you—are you sure? Did you count it?"

"Yes, of course. I got the money today," I said, maybe looking a little surprised. "I counted it when I withdrew it from the bank."

"It makes me a bit uneasy, traveling with that much cash," she said. "But these jewels are just as risky. The money doesn't add much more danger. Put the boxes next to each other. When it's time to leave, you can take off your coat and hide them underneath. I don't want the coachmen to suspect we're carrying anything valuable. Now, can you close the curtains and shut the shutters?"

I had just finished doing that when there was a knock at the door.

"I know who it is," she whispered.

She didn't seem scared. She quietly went to the door and spoke softly with someone for a minute.

"It's my loyal maid," she told me. "She's coming with us. She says we can't leave for about ten more minutes. She's bringing some coffee to the next room."

She peeked into the other room.

"I need to remind her not to bring too much luggage. She always packs too much. Stay here—don't come after me. It's better if she doesn't see you."

She left the room with a look that told me to be careful.

Something about her had changed. Just a little while ago, she seemed so excited. Now, there was a different look on her face—something distant, maybe even suspicious. Her skin was pale. Her eyes had a strange expression. Her voice didn't sound quite the same. Had something gone wrong? Was there danger?

But I quickly told myself not to worry. If something was really wrong, she would have told me. It made sense that she might be getting nervous. After all, the moment we'd been planning for was almost here.

Still, she didn't come back as quickly as I expected.

It's almost impossible to stay calm when you're in my situation. I paced the room, feeling restless. It was a small room. At the far end, there was a door. I opened it, even though I probably shouldn't have.

I listened carefully—nothing. Total silence.

I was so caught up in what was going to happen next that I wasn't thinking clearly about what I was doing right now. That's the only way I can explain all the dumb things I did that night, even though I'm usually careful and not easily fooled.

One of the dumbest things I did was this: instead of closing the door I had opened, which I never should have touched in the first place, I picked up a candle and walked into the next room.

And in that moment, I stumbled upon something completely unexpected—and deeply unsettling.

Chapter XXIII.
A Cup of Coffee

The room had no carpet. On the floor were a bunch of wood shavings and about twenty bricks. But what caught my eye was something lying on a narrow table that I couldn't believe was real.

I walked closer and pulled back a sheet that had barely hidden what was underneath. There was no mistaking it—it was a coffin. On the lid was a metal plate with words in French:

PIERRE DE LA ROCHE ST. AMAND

AGED 23 YEARS

I stepped back, shocked. So the funeral hadn't left yet. The body was still here. I had been misled. That explained why the Countess had seemed so nervous earlier. She should've just told me the truth.

I backed out of the gloomy room and quietly shut the door. Her choice not to trust me had been a big mistake. Sometimes trying to be too careful can make things worse. I had no idea I wasn't supposed to go in there, but I could've run into someone we both wanted to avoid.

Just as these thoughts were racing through my mind, the Countess de St. Alyre came back. She looked at my face and instantly seemed to realize I had discovered something. Her eyes darted quickly to the door.

"Did you see something—something upsetting, dear Richard? Did you leave this room?"

I answered honestly, "Yes," and told her exactly what happened.

"Well, I didn't want to worry you more than I had to," she said. "And it really is horrible. Yes, the body is here. But the Count left about fifteen minutes before I lit the signal lamp for you. The body didn't arrive until eight or ten minutes later. He didn't want the people at Père la Chaise to think the funeral was delayed. He knew Pierre's remains would definitely arrive tonight, even though there was an unexpected delay. And there are reasons why he wants the burial done before tomorrow."

She went on, "The hearse with the coffin will be leaving in ten minutes. Once it's gone, we'll be free to begin our wild and joyful escape. The carriage is waiting in the gateway. And as for this sad and awful thing—" she gave a little shiver, "let's not think about it anymore."

She bolted the door between the rooms, and when she turned back to me, her face showed such sweet, sorry affection that I felt like dropping to my knees before her.

"It's the last time," she said in a soft, pleading voice, "I'll ever hide anything from my brave and beautiful Richard—my hero. Can you forgive me?"

Then came another quiet moment full of emotional whispers, full of affection and promises, spoken gently so no one would overhear.

After a while, she suddenly raised her hand, as if to tell me not to move. Her eyes were locked on mine, and she tilted her head slightly, listening to the door that led to the room with the coffin. She held that still, breathless pose for a few seconds. Then she gave me a small nod, tiptoed to the door, and gently reached her hand back to stop me from following. After listening for a bit, she came back quietly and whispered, "They're moving the coffin—come with me."

She led me into the room where her maid had spoken to her earlier. There was a silver tray with coffee and some delicate, old china cups that looked beautiful to me. Next to it, on another tray, were tiny liqueur glasses and a flask of something sweet—it turned out to be a drink called noyau.

"I'll serve you," she said with a smile. "I'm your maid tonight. You have to let me take care of you, or I'll think you haven't forgiven me."

She poured coffee into one of the cups and handed it to me with her left hand. Her right arm wrapped lovingly around my shoulder, and she gently played with my hair as she whispered, "Drink this—I'll have some soon too."

The coffee was excellent. When I finished, she handed me one of the liqueur glasses. I drank that too.

"Let's go back to the other room," she said. "By now, those people must be gone, and it'll be safer there for now."

"You're in charge. Whatever you say, I'll do—now and forever," I said, completely swept up in emotion.

I admit now, I was talking like one of those overly romantic heroes from French novels. Looking back, I'm embarrassed by how dramatic I was with the Countess.

"Here, one more little glass of noyau," she said cheerfully. The sadness and tension from before had vanished. Just like that, she seemed lighthearted again. She ran off and came back with another tiny glass. I took it with some more over-the-top words and sipped it.

I kissed her hand, then her lips. I looked into her beautiful eyes and kissed her again.

"You call me Richard. What name should I use for my beautiful goddess?" I asked.

"Call me Eugenie. That's my real name. Let's be honest with each other—if your love is as real as mine."

"Eugenie!" I said with passion, thrilled just to say her name.

We talked more about how much I wanted to begin our escape. But just as I was speaking, something strange happened. It didn't feel like fainting. It's hard to describe—it was like something in my brain tightened, almost as if the space around it had suddenly stiffened.

"Richard! What's wrong?" she cried, looking panicked. "Are you sick? Please, sit—sit in this chair!"

She helped me into a chair. I didn't resist. I knew this feeling too well. I was slipping into that awful frozen state I'd experienced before, during my nighttime drive to Paris with the Marquis. I couldn't speak, couldn't close my eyes, couldn't move. In just a few seconds, I was completely paralyzed.

At first, Eugenie panicked. She screamed my name, shook me, lifted my arm and let it fall, begging me to move, even just a little. She swore if I didn't respond, she would kill herself.

But after a couple of minutes, she suddenly went quiet. Her whole mood changed. Calm and focused, she picked up a candle and held it in front of me. Her face was pale, but now she just looked serious and intense. She slowly moved the candle in front of my eyes, studying my reaction closely.

Then she set the candle down and rang a small bell several times, sharply. She brought both boxes—hers with the jewels, and mine with the money—and placed them side by side on the table. I watched as she carefully locked the door leading to the room where I had just drunk the coffee.

Chapter XXIV.
Hope

She had barely set my heavy box down—it clearly took effort—when the door to the room with the coffin suddenly opened, and someone unexpected walked in.

It was Count de St. Alyre. I had been told he was on his way to Père la Chaise, so seeing him here shocked me. For a moment, he stood framed in the doorway, surrounded by darkness like a shadowy portrait. He looked small and frail in deep black mourning clothes, with a pair of black gloves in one hand and a hat wrapped in black fabric in the other.

When he wasn't speaking, his face twitched and moved like he was holding back nerves or rage. He looked both wicked and afraid.

"Well, my dear Eugénie? So, sweetheart—hmm? Is everything going as planned?" he asked.

"Yes," she replied in a quiet, serious voice. "But you and Planard made a mistake. You shouldn't have left that door open."

She said this sternly. "He went in and looked around wherever he wanted. It's lucky he didn't lift the lid of the coffin."

"Planard should have taken care of that," the Count snapped. "I can't be everywhere!" He took a few fast steps toward me and held his glasses up to his eyes.

"Monsieur Beckett!" he shouted a couple of times. "Hey! Don't you recognize me?"

He came closer, leaned over me, shook my hand, and let it drop again. "It's working beautifully, my little darling. When did it start?"

The Countess stood next to him, staring at me with a hard, steady gaze. The way both of them looked at me sent chills down my spine.

She glanced at the mantel where a clock ticked quietly.

"Four... five... six and a half minutes," she said slowly and coldly.

"Brava! Bravissima! My queen! My little Venus! My Joan of Arc! My perfect woman!" the Count gushed.

He smiled with nasty excitement as he reached backward, searching for her hand. But she stepped away slightly, clearly avoiding his touch.

"Come on, my dear, let's count this. What is it? A wallet? Or what?"

"That," she said, pointing at the box with a look of disgust.

"Ah! Let's see—let's count. Let's open it up," he said, starting to unbuckle the leather straps with trembling fingers. "We must count— yes, but—where's the key? This cursed lock! Where is it? Where's the key?"

He stood there, twitching, hands shaking.

"I don't have it. How could I? It's in his pocket, of course," she replied.

In a flash, the old man was digging through my pockets. He yanked out everything, including the keys.

I was still trapped in the same frozen state I'd experienced on the drive to Paris with the Marquis. I knew now they were robbing me. I didn't fully understand the Countess's role in all of this—was she in on it the whole time, or surprised by his sudden return? But it was becoming clearer by the second.

I couldn't move my eyes even slightly, but even so, I could see nearly everything in the room. From where I was, I could observe the entire scene clearly.

The Count found the key. He opened the leather cover, then unlocked the iron-bound box. He dumped its contents onto the table.

"Rolls of a hundred Napoleons. One, two, three... yes. Write down a thousand. One, two... another thousand. Write!" He went on like this, quickly counting the gold. Then he moved on to the paper money.

"Ten thousand francs. Write it down. Another ten thousand—do you have that? Again—another ten thousand. Ugh, these large bills are a pain. Smaller ones would've been better. Bolt that door—Planard will freak out if he sees this amount. Why didn't you ask for smaller notes? Never mind, write—another ten thousand, and another."

I had to sit there, paralyzed, as I watched and heard them count every coin and bill of my fortune, crystal clear in my mind, even though I couldn't move a muscle.

Once it was all counted, he carefully put everything back into the box, locked it, placed it into the leather case, and then opened a hidden cabinet in the wall. He put the jewel box and my strongbox inside, locked the door, and turned back to complain bitterly about Planard again.

He unbolted a door, peeked into the dark room beyond, listened, then came back. He was clearly nervous.

"I kept ten thousand francs for Planard," he said, patting his vest pocket.

"Do you think that's enough for him?" the lady asked.

"Enough? Curse him!" the Count shouted. "He has no conscience. I'll swear to him that's half of it."

They both came to look at me again. The Count muttered, compared his watch to the clock, then started pacing and complaining again. The Countess sat quietly, no longer looking at me. She gazed off across the room, her face in profile—and now she looked entirely different. Harsh, cold, like a witch. Any last bit of hope I had faded completely. Her mask had dropped. I now felt sure they planned to kill me. But why delay?

I can't fully explain the horror of those moments. It felt like being trapped in a real nightmare, where the people tormenting you hold your life in their hands and choose not to end it just yet, enjoying your fear.

And then, while I lay there frozen in terror, the door to the room with the coffin opened again.

The Marquis d'Harmonville stepped inside.

Chapter XXV.
Despair

For a second, I felt a flash of hope—quick and shaky. But then I heard voices, and my heart sank.

"Finally, Planard, you're here," said the Count, grabbing him by both arms and pulling him closer. "Look—just look at him. Everything's gone perfectly so far. Want me to hold the candle for you?"

My supposed friend, the Marquis d'Harmonville—Planard, or whoever he really was—walked over to me while removing his gloves and stuffing them into his pocket.

"Move the candle a little closer," he said. He leaned down and looked carefully at my face. He touched my forehead, brushed his hand across it, then stared into my eyes.

"Well, doctor?" whispered the Count.

"How much did you give him?" Planard asked, now acting like a doctor.

"Seventy drops," the woman answered.

"In the hot coffee?"

"Yes. Sixty in the coffee and ten more in the liqueur."

Her voice was cold and calm, but I noticed it tremble slightly. No matter how heartless people seem, it takes a long time to completely silence their guilt.

The doctor stayed calm. He checked my eyes again, felt my wrist, and muttered, "No pulse."

Then he held something thin and gold-colored near my lips, making sure his own breath didn't get in the way.

"Yes," he said quietly to himself.

He opened my shirt and used a stethoscope to listen to my chest. He moved it around, checking carefully.

"No signs of breathing," he murmured.

Then he said louder, "Seventy drops, maybe ten lost, should keep him out for six and a half hours—that's plenty. In the carriage, I only used thirty, and it worked fast. His brain is very sensitive. We can't kill him. You're sure it was just seventy?"

"I'm sure," she said firmly.

"If he dies, they'll find the poison during the autopsy. That would ruin everything. If there's even a little doubt, we should use the stomach pump."

"Eugénie, please, be honest," begged the Count.

"I am. I'm completely sure," she replied.

"How long ago exactly? I told you to check the time."

"I did. The minute hand was right under Cupid's foot."

"Then it should last around seven hours. When he wakes up, there won't be a trace of it left in his stomach."

At least I knew now—they didn't plan to kill me. Not yet, anyway. But the fear of dying while fully awake and unable to move was terrifying. You can't really understand it unless you've felt it yourself.

Still, I didn't get why they were being so careful if they were just robbing me.

"You're leaving France?" Planard asked.

"Yes, tomorrow," the Count replied.

"And where are you going?"

"I haven't decided."

"Not going to tell your friend?"

"I can't. I honestly don't know. This plan didn't work out as well as I hoped."

"We'll figure that out later."

"It's time to lay him down," said the Count, pointing at me.

"Yes. Let's hurry. Is his night-shirt and cap ready?"

"They're ready," said the Count.

"Madame," said the doctor, turning to the lady and giving a small bow, "it's time for you to leave."

She walked into the room where I'd had the drugged coffee. I didn't see her again.

The Count came back with some folded clothes and locked both doors. Then he and Planard quickly started undressing me. They worked fast and silently.

They put a long nightshirt on me that reached past my feet and tied a soft sleeping cap under my chin. It looked more like something a woman would wear.

I assumed they'd just leave me to wake up in bed while they ran off with the money. That seemed like the best I could hope for—but I was wrong.

The Count and Planard went into the next room. I heard them whispering and dragging something heavy. Then came a loud rumbling sound.

They came back, walking backward as they pulled something large across the floor. I couldn't see what it was at first.

Then I saw it—and my blood ran cold.

They had brought in the coffin from the other room. It was now lying flat on the floor, right next to my chair. Planard lifted the lid.

The coffin was empty.

Chapter XXVI.
Catastrophe

"Those horses look strong, and we'll switch them along the way," said Planard. "Give the drivers a gold coin or two. We've got to finish this in three hours and fifteen minutes. Now, help me—I'll lift him so we can place his feet right. You keep them together and pull the white shirt down over them."

A moment later, Planard had me standing at the foot of the coffin. He gently lowered me into it until I was lying flat. Then he arranged my arms at my sides, smoothed the fabric over my chest, and adjusted the folds of the burial clothes. He stepped back to check everything and seemed satisfied.

The Count, who liked things done just right, quickly folded up my clothes and locked them inside one of the closets built into the wall.

Now I understood everything—and it was terrifying. This coffin was meant for me. The funeral for St. Amand was fake, a trick to stop people from asking questions. I had signed all the papers, paid the fees, and even given the burial instructions myself—thinking I was helping with someone else's funeral. But I was actually arranging my own.

Their plan was to bury me alive, still unconscious from the drug. I would wake up hours later, trapped in the coffin, buried under heavy dirt, alone in the dark, and die the most horrifying death imaginable.

Even if someone later dug up the coffin, nothing would show I'd been poisoned or hurt. It would look like a normal death.

And I had made it worse by trying to disappear on purpose. I had written letters to people back home in England telling them not to expect anything from me for at least three weeks.

I had felt so proud and excited, and now I was facing death. I tried to pray, but all I could think about was fear, judgment, and endless pain.

There's no way to describe everything I felt. The fear, the regret, the horror—it was beyond words. But I'll tell you what happened next. I remember every second clearly.

"The undertaker's men are here," said the Count.

"Not yet," said Planard. "Let's put the lid on first. You take the bottom, I've got the top."

I didn't need to guess what they were doing. A few seconds later, the lid slid shut above me, cutting off all light. Everything became muffled. Then came the slow, dreadful sound of screws turning—one after another. Each one felt like it was sealing me in forever.

What happened next I only found out later.

After they screwed the lid shut, the two men cleaned up the room to make it look calm and normal. The Count didn't want anything to seem rushed or suspicious. Once the coffin was positioned perfectly on the floor, Planard said he would go call the men to carry it to the hearse.

The Count put on black gloves and held a white handkerchief. He looked like the perfect grieving relative. He stood behind the head of the coffin, waiting for the men to arrive.

Planard came in first, walking through the room where the coffin had been before. He seemed more confident now.

"Count," he said, walking in with six other men, "I'm sorry to interrupt, but we have a problem. This is Monsieur Carmaignac from the police. He says there's been a report that a lot of smuggled English goods have been hidden in this area—and some might be in your house. I told him that's definitely not true, and that you'd be happy to let him search the place."

"Of course," the Count said loudly, but his face was pale. "Thank you, friend, for saying so. My home and keys are at his service. Just tell me what he's looking for."

"I'm not allowed to say," Carmaignac replied. "I've been told to do a full search. This warrant gives me permission."

"Sir," Planard added, trying to help, "maybe you could let the Count attend his cousin's funeral first? The coffin is right here," he said, pointing to the nameplate, "and the hearse is already waiting outside."

"I'm sorry," said Carmaignac firmly. "That's not possible. I have to follow orders. The Count may be innocent, but I have to act like he's not. You'd be surprised where people hide things. For all I know, someone could be using that coffin to smuggle something."

"That coffin holds my cousin, Monsieur Pierre de St. Amand," the Count said proudly.

"Oh? You've seen the body?"

"Seen him? Yes, too many times," the Count said, clearly nervous.

"I meant the body itself."

The Count quickly glanced at Planard before replying.

"N-no, not exactly… only for a moment."

Planard gave the Count another quick look.

"But you saw him clearly enough to recognize him, right?" he asked with a slight edge to his voice.

"Of course—of course I did," the Count said quickly. "Right away. Perfectly. What? Not recognize Pierre de St. Amand? No, no—poor man—I knew him too well for that."

"I'm looking for something that could be hidden in a small space," said Monsieur Carmaignac. "Servants can be very clever. Let's open the coffin."

"Excuse me, sir," said the Count firmly, stepping to the side of the coffin and stretching out his arm to block it. "I can't allow such an insult—such a disrespect."

"There will be no disrespect," Carmaignac replied calmly. "Just lifting the lid. You can stay in the room. If everything is as we hope, you'll have one last chance to see your dear relative."

"But sir, I just can't allow it."

"But I must," said Carmaignac.

"Besides, the tool broke when the last screw was fastened," the Count added. "I give you my word—there's nothing in the coffin but the body."

"I'm sure the Count believes that," said Carmaignac, "but he doesn't know the sneaky tricks servants can use. Philippe—open the coffin."

The Count kept protesting, but Philippe, a bald, dirty-faced man who looked like a blacksmith, set down a leather tool bag. He looked at the screws, picked at them with his fingernail, chose the right tool, and in no time had them all loosened. The lid came off.

Light spilled in, and I saw it—light I thought I'd never see again. But I couldn't move my eyes; I was still in a frozen, cataleptic state. Since I'd been laid nearly upright in the coffin, I continued to stare straight ahead, now at the ceiling.

Carmaignac leaned over me with a curious frown, clearly not recognizing me. Oh, how I wished I could cry out! I saw the little Count's cruel face staring at me from the other side. The false Marquis looked down too, though not as directly. A few other faces hovered behind them.

"I see, I see," said Carmaignac, stepping back. "Nothing unusual in there."

"Please ask your man to put the lid back and screw it down again," said the Count, trying to sound firm. "And really, the funeral must go on. These men don't get paid much for working at night—it's unfair to keep them waiting."

"You'll be leaving very soon," said Carmaignac. "But first, I have some things to do regarding this coffin."

The Count turned toward the door and saw a police officer standing there. Two or three more officers had also come into the room. The Count was visibly shaken—it was becoming too much for him.

"If this gentleman won't let me attend my cousin's funeral," he said, "then Planard, I'll ask you to go instead."

"In just a moment," said Carmaignac coolly. "First, I need the key to that cabinet."

He pointed straight at the one where my clothes had just been locked.

"I—I don't mind," said the Count nervously. "But they haven't been opened in years. I'll tell someone to look for the key."

"No need," said Carmaignac. "Philippe, try your skeleton keys. I want it opened."

Philippe got the cabinet open. Carmaignac pulled out the clothes that had only been placed inside a few minutes ago.

"Whose clothes are these?" he asked.

"I don't know," said the Count. "I've never looked in that cabinet. A servant named Lablais had the key. I fired him a year ago. I haven't seen it open in ten years. Those must be his."

Carmaignac held up some visiting cards and a handkerchief marked "R.B."

"Looks like they were stolen from someone named Beckett—R. Beckett. This card says 'Mr. Beckett, Berkeley Square.' And here's a watch and a bunch of seals—one marked with 'R.B.' That servant Lablais must have been a real thief!"

"Exactly right," the Count agreed.

Carmaignac narrowed his eyes. "Or maybe he didn't steal them from some stranger. Maybe he took them from the man in the coffin. Maybe that man isn't St. Amand at all—but Mr. Beckett. Because guess what? The watch is still ticking."

He turned and pointed at the coffin.

"I don't think he's dead. I think he's drugged. And for robbing him and planning to murder him, I arrest you—Nicolas de la Marque, Count de St. Alyre."

In the next moment, the old man was under arrest. I could hear his rough voice break into wild shouting, switching between begging, threatening, and screaming. One moment he was croaking out curses, the next he was shouting to God to judge everyone fairly. He kept lying and raving as the officers took him away. They placed him in the same coach as his beautiful but heartless partner, who had already been arrested. Two policemen sat beside them, and the carriage quickly sped off toward the prison at the Conciergerie.

Suddenly, two more voices joined the scene. One was from Colonel Gaillarde, who had been held back until now but was loudly trying to take credit for everything. The other was from my cheerful friend Whistlewick, who had come to help prove who I really was.

I'll explain in a moment how this whole awful plan to steal my money and end my life was finally uncovered. But first, let me tell you what happened to me. I was placed in a hot bath, under the watch of Planard—a man just as evil as the rest of them, but now helping the police. After that, they put me in a warm bed with the window open. These simple steps saved my life. In about three hours, I woke up. Without this help, I would've stayed unconscious for nearly seven hours.

The criminals behind this plot were extremely careful and smart. Their victims, like me, were tricked into helping with the very plan meant to destroy them. That's what made the scheme so dangerous—and so effective.

Of course, the police began a full investigation. They searched the cemetery at Père la Chaise and opened several graves. Most of the bodies were too old and decomposed to identify. But one was recognized. In that case, the funeral notice had been signed and paid for by Gabriel Gaillarde—someone the cemetery clerk remembered dealing with.

That whole funeral had been fake. The name on the tombstone and coffin belonged to a made-up person. In reality, Gabriel Gaillarde himself had been buried there under that false name. The same trick they had used on him was the one they had planned for me.

The way they figured out the body was his was strange. Gabriel had been injured years earlier when a horse threw him. He lost an eye, several teeth, and broke his leg just above the ankle. He'd tried to keep these injuries a secret. But the glass eye was still in the skull—just slightly out of place—and the man who had made it recognized his own work.

Even more convincing were the teeth. A well-known Paris dentist had made a custom gold plate to fit Gabriel's mouth. He had kept the mold because the injury was so unusual. When they compared the gold plate found in the skull to the old mold, it matched exactly. The leg bone also showed signs of the old break, matching Gabriel's known injury perfectly.

Colonel Gaillarde, Gabriel's younger brother, had been furious about Gabriel's disappearance—especially about the money, which he believed should've come to him. He had long suspected that Count de St. Alyre and the beautiful woman he called the Countess had scammed his brother. He even began to suspect something worse, though at first it was more anger than actual evidence.

Eventually, the Colonel stumbled onto a clue that put him on the right track. Around the same time, Planard realized the whole gang—including himself—was about to be caught. So he made a deal to save himself. He agreed to tell everything and helped the police set up the surprise visit to the Château de la Carque—just in time to catch the criminals red-handed.

I don't need to go into all the careful work the police did to gather the evidence for the case. They even brought in a skilled doctor who could have given expert testimony if Planard hadn't already come forward.

As you can imagine, my trip to Paris didn't go quite the way I had hoped. Instead of a fun visit, I ended up being the main witness in a major court case. That might sound exciting, but it came with a lot of unwanted attention. After barely escaping with my life—what my friend Whistlewick called a "close call"—I expected that people would be interested in my story. But instead, I became a joke. People laughed at me, called me names like "fool" and "donkey," and I even appeared in some mocking cartoons. I was treated like a minor celebrity—but not in a good way.

I left Paris as soon as I could, without even stopping by the Marquis d'Harmonville's country house like I had planned.

The Marquis got away without punishment. The Count, however, was executed. As for the beautiful Eugenie, she was sentenced to six years in prison, though it seemed like her looks helped reduce the penalty.

Colonel Gaillarde got back some of his brother's stolen money from what was left of the Count's and "Countess's" estate. Between the money and the Count's execution, the Colonel was in a great mood. Instead of challenging me to a duel over the injury I gave him, he shook my hand and said he considered the blow from my walking stick to be part of an honest fight—even if it wasn't quite by the rules.

There are just two more things to mention. First, the bricks found in the coffin room had been packed in straw to mimic the weight of a body. This was to stop anyone from getting suspicious when the empty coffin first arrived at the château. Second, the Countess's amazing diamond jewelry turned out to be fake. A gem expert said it was worth about five pounds—basically the kind of costume jewelry a stage actress might wear.

It turns out the Countess had been a skilled actress on the smaller stages of Paris years before. The Count found her there and made her his main partner in crime.

She was the one who, in disguise, had gone through my documents during the carriage ride to Paris. She had also played the fortune-teller in the palanquin at the ball in Versailles. That strange event was designed to pull me deeper into the Countess's story in case I started to lose interest. It was also meant to fool other targets—but we don't need to talk about them now.

The body used in that event was real, provided by someone who sold corpses to medical schools in Paris. It added mystery without real risk and helped keep the magician's reputation alive among the curious crowd.

After all this, I spent the rest of the summer and fall traveling between Switzerland and Italy. As the saying goes, I was a sadder man—if not a wiser one.

A lot of what haunted me afterward came from how shaken my nerves were. But deeper feelings stuck with me, too. That experience changed the way I lived. It took years, but in the end, it led me to a better, more thoughtful life. I'm truly grateful to God for teaching me such a powerful and painful lesson early in life about the danger of sin.

The End

Thank You for Reading

Dear Reader,

We hope this timeless classic has sparked your imagination and enriched your literary journey. Now that you've turned the final page, we want to share a vision for the future of reading—one where every classic you've ever wanted to explore is at your fingertips, in a format that best suits your life.

We'd like to invite you to gain immediate, unlimited digital & audiobook access to hundreds of the most treasured literary classics ever written—along with the option to secure deluxe paperback, hardcover & box set editions at printing cost. Together, we can spark a new global literary renaissance alongside our small, independent publishing house called "The Library of Alexandria."

Thousands of years ago, the Library of Alexandria stood as a beacon of knowledge—until it was lost to history. We aim to reignite that spirit of preservation and discovery right now, in the modern age—only this time, it's accessible to all, in every language and every format.

Picture a world where every timeless classic, novel, poem, or philosophical treatise is not only available to read but also updated for today's readers—modernized, translated into any language or dialect, and ready to enjoy in any format you choose, whether that is in an eBook, audiobook, paperback, or deluxe hardcover & box set version a printing cost.

By joining our movement to rebuild the modern Library of Alexandria, you become part of an unprecedented mission to offer:

- **Unlimited Audiobook & eBook Access to the Greatest Classics of All Time**

  Instantly explore thousands of legendary works, from Plato and Shakespeare to Jane Austen and Leo Tolstoy. All are instantly ready to read or listen to, giving you a complete literary universe at your fingertips.

- **Paperback & Deluxe Editions at Printing Costs:**

  Purchase any title in a paperback, deluxe hardbound, or deluxe boxset edition at printing costs, shipped right to your doorstep. Curate your personal library of Alexandria with editions worthy of display—crafted to last, designed to captivate, and delivered straight to your door.

- **Modern translations for Contemporary Readers in all languages and dialects**

  Discover a vast selection of classics reimagined in clear, current language—no more struggling with outdated phrases or obscure references. Next to the original versions, we aim to offer translations in as many languages and dialects as possible.

  As we continue our translation efforts and add new languages, readers everywhere can connect with these works as if they were written today. By bridging linguistic divides, you're contributing to ensuring that these timeless stories become more meaningful, accessible, and inspiring for people across the globe.

- **Your Personal Library of Alexandria:**

  Over the months and years, you'll curate a unique physical archive of classics—each volume a testament to your taste, curiosity, and love of knowledge. It's not just about owning books—it's about curating a cultural legacy you'll cherish and pass down for generations to come.

- **Join a Global Literary Renaissance:**

  Your support fuels an ongoing mission: allowing us to reinvest in offering deluxe print editions (including special boxsets) at their true cost, broaden the range of available formats and translations, and extend the reach of these works to new audiences worldwide. By joining today, you're not just preserving a legacy of masterpieces; you set in motion a powerful wave of literary accessibility.

  We are more than a publisher—we're a movement, and we can't do it alone. Your support lets us scale our mission, preserving and reimagining history's greatest works for tomorrow's readers.

Become a Torchbearer of knowledge.

Thank you for picking up this book and allowing us into your literary journey. As you turn the pages, know that you're part of something larger: a global effort to keep these stories alive, share their wisdom across borders and generations, and spark a true cultural revival for the modern era.

If this resonates with you—please consider taking the next step by visiting:

www.libraryofalexandria.com

With gratitude and a shared love of knowledge,

The Modern Library of Alexandria Team

Visit:

www.libraryofalexandria.com

Or scan the code below: